.

God's Focus on the Fatherless

God's Focus on the Fatherless

A Lens to Inform Spiritual Impact in the Local Church

Dwight David Croy

WIPF & STOCK · Eugene, Oregon

GOD'S FOCUS ON THE FATHERLESS
A Lens to Inform Spiritual Impact in the Local Church

Wipf & Stock
An Imprint of Wipf and Stock Publishers
199 W. 8th Ave., Suite 3
Eugene, OR 97401

www.wipfandstock.com

PAPERBACK ISBN 13: 978-1-4982-3545-7
HARDCOVER ISBN 13: 978-1-4982-3547-1

Manufactured in the U.S.A.   03/28/2016

All Scripture quotations, unless otherwise indicated, are taken from the
New International Version of the Bible.

Dedicated to my loving wife, Karen, who has kept the home fires burning, maintained family traditions, and is my prayerful guardian through all the thirty-plus years of military hardships of separation, odd hours, and crisis ministry

God providing peace for sinners: It's something God does for us and not what we do for Him. You see it's not God—who needs to be turned around. It's not God who needs to be reconciled—it's man.

—PASTOR DAVID W. CROY,
COMMUNION SERVICE, JUNE 4, 1989

Contents

Preface

The study of the plight of the fatherless as seen through God's vision and perspective based on God's name and character for the purpose of outreach is motivated by several personal factors. This study grows out of generations past, present and future. My passion for reaching the fatherless is spurred on by my father's experience growing up, my experience in ministry, and a spirit of thankful admiration for saints of God who have not only been living models of faithfulness for me, but have invested into my walk with the Lord.

My dad, who is with his heavenly Father now, lost his dad as a boy of eight years old. He also lost his mother who was committed to a mental institution at about the same time of losing his dad. The social stigma resulting from his mom's reality was so strong, so shameful in its day, that it was rarely if ever spoken of; and I did not learn of it until my adult years. Despite the environmental chaos of being raised by other relatives, moving around the country, and having no steady father figure, my dad was touched by the saving grace of God in the Army and went on to raise a family of six children in a committed marriage of fifty-plus years. My dad poured his life into the church and drew great strength from God's ecclesiastical program. The dynamic strength of the church is found when the people of God follow Jesus Christ in his great commission "to tell the Good News to all the earth;" and this my dad not only did with great passion, but he also very much enjoyed it. My dad's great passion, however, was not an easy one. The administration, organization, and structure of the local church were not a source of strength. As he said many times, he learned that part by plenty of "hard knocks." He was a shepherd of God's flock faithfully throughout all the hard and easy times of a church family's spiritual growth.

The second motivating factor for the study of God's vision for the fatherless is my twenty-five plus years of ministry as an Army chaplain. Although there are good news stories of the fatherless, there are many more that are devastating. If a posttraumatic stress element to professional pastoral counseling in the chaplaincy could be identified, it is the predicaments of multiple young men and women who desire and thirst for a strong male guide in their life. The death of one's father is hard enough to explain to a child, but a dad who chooses to stay away is even harder. After a quarter of a century, I am convinced that local church ministries are the answer to such pain—not national, international, or government institutions. God's directive to meet the needs of the fatherless (orphan), widow, and alien provides insight and directives as to how the local church is to approach intentional ministry.

My final reason for applying God's fatherless vision as a framework to the outreach of the local church is a passion sustained by the saints of God who have gone before me. They have given their all as a "living sacrifice" to encourage me to grow in the Lord. My prayer warriors have been many. Their battles in the spiritual realm on my behalf are yet unseen and unrewarded. The power of their prayers was evident when, at the end of my resources, God empowered me to go further. The many saints of God are the embodiment of his program; they are the church. Whatever comes of this study, I pray that it will impact the church to multiply God's glory and grace in the world the way that he desires.

The primary source for this body of research is the Word of God; focusing on the theme of "fatherlessness" throughout Scripture. Peer-reviewed journals and respected authors are also cited in the academic portion of the study, whereas, life experience, or autoethnography, is relevant for the creation of the following book. This is a nonprescriptive study guide for local churches to assist in rethinking structural and administrative systems in order to be more effective in outreach. Fatherless elements or factors set the framework and serve as a lens through which local church leadership can evaluate their own God-given ministries.

Acknowledgments

Gratitude overflows from my heart to my family, especially my wife, Karen, who for thirty-three years has encouraged me. I am eternally grateful for my prayerful mom, Wanda Croy, who led me to the Lord at a young age. Thank you to both my daughter, Amber Dierking, and my cousin, Daren Croy, for taking the time to read and reread the manuscript for more and more clarity. Mandy and Jonathan Croy, and Adam Dierking have shown loving support, encouragement, and patience with "my nose in the books." First Baptist Church of Medford, Oregon, will always be my home church in my heart and the multiple saints who encouraged my steps of faith and leadership. Both Multnomah University and Denver Seminary gave me the formal foundational building blocks built on the Chief Cornerstone to minister in the local church and go into the military chaplaincy full time. Upon retiring from the United States Army after twenty-five years of service as a chaplain, the pursuit and journey of a Doctor of Ministry has been a source of joy and spiritual growth. The journey is a small taste of heaven to come when God gathers the saints from all time and four corners of the earth. My cohort have been instructive, challenging, encouraging builders of my spiritual life. George Fox University has a great program and puts together diverse cohorts for maximum learning, fellowship, and accountability. The cohort expands one's view of the church and presents new outreach challenges. It is my belief that the program exceeds what they pray for in educational professionalism and unknown reverberations will be seen in eternity. Finally and not least, my heart is thankful to the great throng of saints who have gone before me. Among them are people who have poured their life into me and continue to have a spiritual effect upon this earth.

God's plan is large and beyond earthly comprehension and I look forward to the eternal postscript before his throne when we start to comprehend it.

1

God's Fatherless Focus

But You, O God, do see trouble and grief; you consider it to take it in hand. The victim commits himself to you; you are the helper of the fatherless.

—PSALM 10:14

Nothing in all creation is hidden from God's sight. Everything is uncovered and laid bare before the eyes of him to whom we must give account.

—HEBREWS 4:13

Skip was in the top bunk. Buckled over, holding his stomach, and wincing in obvious pain. The church camp pastor had been notified along with the camp nurse. Through a series of questions from the nurse we found out that he had stomach pains all week. He had told no one. It was Friday and camp was almost over. The camp of three hundred or more teens would be going home Saturday morning after breakfast. Skip told the staff that he knew there was a chance he would have to go home early; he did not want to. It was so obvious that he was having the time of his life. As his camp counselor I noticed that he initiated speaking to me and other leaders in engaging conversation and activities all through the week. We found out later that Skip was having so much fun and enjoying the loving Christian environment, he was hiding something that could send him home. The last thing he wanted to do was go home. It turned out that he had appendicitis and needed to go to a hospital right away. Skip came from a well-off family with lots of money. His dad was notified, and he sent a helicopter to the camp. From across the baseball field, I watched as the nurse helped him into the helicopter. There was a pilot and another large man there to help. When the nurse came back, I asked if that was his father. With her eyes to the ground she said simply, "No." In that moment, as a spiritual leadership team for these young people, we were sad. Here was a child with a father, yet no father. At the same time, as I thought back over the week, I was overjoyed. We, as ministers of God, were able to fill a void, share our joy in Christ, and show the love of an everlasting father. We did it accidently, by just being available. But what if we did it intentionally? So often in the Bible, God exhorts us to pay attention to the fatherless and chooses to frame our relationship to him in the context of the intimacy of a father and his children. Perhaps we are to see what it takes to reach out to the fatherless and apply it to all the ministries of the church. What would ministry in the local church look like if we purposely put Father God principles in it? What is God looking at when he sees the fatherless? What does his heart expect from us?

Where Is "Fatherlessness" in the Bible?

Insight and discernment concerning fatherlessness comes from forty-three passages of Scripture, forty-two in the Old Testament and one in the New Testament. (See table 1). The English transliteration of the Hebrew word for fatherless is "yathom," a masculine noun with a short definition of "orphan." *Strong's Concordance* defines the word, "From an unused root meaning to be lonely; a bereaved person—fatherless (child) orphan." An overwhelming majority of the references to the "fatherless" (orphan; noun; masculine), are contained in the Old Testament. The context shows both "fatherless" and "orphan" to be a correct meaning of the Hebrew word. One may draw the conclusion that orphans are the very picture of weakness and vulnerability.

The term "fatherlessness" is a repeated term throughout Scripture, contained in the commands from God in the law. It is God's expectation that his holy people have a vision and a will for taking care of the "fatherless."

1) Exodus 22:22	16) Job 24:3	31) Isaiah 1:23
2) Exodus 22:24	17) Job 24:9	32) Isaiah 9:17
3) Deuteronomy 10:18	18) Job 29:12	33) Isaiah 10:2
4) Deuteronomy 14:29	19) Job 31:17	34) Jeremiah 5:28
5) Deuteronomy 16:11	20) Job 31:21	35) Jeremiah 7:6
6) Deuteronomy 16:14	21) Psalm 10:14	36) Jeremiah 22:3
7) Deuteronomy 24:17	22) Psalm 10:18	37) Jeremiah 49:11
8) Deuteronomy 24:19	23) Psalm 68:5	38) Lamentations 5:3
9) Deuteronomy 24:20	24) Psalm 82:3	39) Ezekiel 22:7
10) Deuteronomy 24:21	25) Psalm 94:6	40) Hosea 14:3
11) Deuteronomy 26:12	26) Psalm 109:9	41) Zechariah 7:10
12) Deuteronomy 26:13	27) Psalm 109:12	42) Malachi 3:5
13) Deuteronomy 27:19	28) Psalm 146:9	43) James 1:27
14) Job 6:27	29) Proverbs 23:10	
15) Job 22:9	30) Isaiah 1:17	

Table 1. Scripture Passages with the Word "Fatherless"

Although the term "fatherless" is scarce in the New Testament, important observations can be made from Jesus Christ who came to fulfill the law. Jesus Christ lived out God's heart by addressing the "least of these" as a repeated pattern of a pure life. God reached us, the broken of this world, through Jesus Christ. Jesus Christ commissioned us to do the same. Based on his reach to us, we are to turn around and reach out in like manner to the brokenness embodied in fatherlessness that is evident in our local communities.

The Principled Expanse of Fatherlessness

Throughout this book the "fatherless" will often be interchangeable with the disenfranchised, the aborted child, the voiceless, the widow, the orphan, the alien, the prisoner, the mentally ill, the alcoholic, the elderly, the bedridden, and the stranger. To narrow the study, I have chosen the alignment of seeing the fatherless as much as I can through God's way of seeing, with his concerns for the fatherless. The forty-three scriptures referring to the fatherless and the orphan will be cited throughout. Please note that God refers to other desolate people groups as well. God has called attention to these people groups to define his outreach to the world. The lens of the fatherless also gives us insight to the sensitivity of his heart. Therefore, we need to give the outreach principles of the fatherless our full attention.

Descriptive vs. Prescriptive

Have you ever noticed that God does not tell us how to peel fruit? Throughout this life God has given us, we have never felt micromanaged by him. He is faithful to model, to repeat principles, and to reveal his person through the Word of God. He gives us great latitude and opportunities to glorify him through the discernment of the broken relationships around us and our choices can be worship as we delight in him. He delights in our creativity, and encourages our loving outreach to the world as his personal reflections. The next few chapters will explore the forty-three passages of Scripture to extract overarching principles and what is expected from a loving God reflected in the Christian community. Our emphasis will be on the long threads of consistent truth that run through the "fatherless" Scripture passages. God's dominant principled lenses concerning the fatherless will inform our view of ministry outreach.

Outreach Flowing through the Fatherless Lens

This study is not about the one specific facet of or solution to fatherlessness; there are many excellent ministries in this area of the disenfranchised such as adoption, mentorship, church ministry models, specific counseling programs, etc. This study focuses instead on God's vision of reaching out to the fatherless and how that vision informs our outreach in all areas of ministry. Out of this study a lens of priorities will emerge for ministry as a whole. Discernment for greater specificity in ministry will come into view as we align our eyesight with God's.

When one starts to address ministry needs, the humanness in us tends to overreach or "bleed" for the one destitute group. Robert Lupton, founder and president of FCS Urban Ministries (Focused Community Strategies), says it in a concentrated way in his potent little book, *Toxic Charity*:

> Doing *for* rather than doing *with* those in need is the norm. Add to it the combination of patronizing pity and unintended superiority, and charity becomes toxic.[1]

As well-meaning, sincere people get involved, they actually start to believe that they are the only one that can see this specific pain in the world. For people who give of themselves regularly, this is a kind of "snow blindness." It prevents you from seeing a bigger picture, one that comes from the heart of God. The bigger picture is seeing the destitute God's way which is greater than our limited created sight. For the church, goodness or good ministry proceeds from the being or nature of God. It is because of who God is that we that can navigate toward outreach ministry that reflects his heart. Tim Challies, editor of *Discerning Reader* (www. discerningreader.com) emphasizes God's help in discernment:

---

1. Lupton, *Toxic Charity*, 35.

While the Bible makes it clear that discernment relates to decision making, my studies of this topic have led me to see that a definition that goes little further than this is simply too narrow, for biblical discernment looks beyond the will of God to the *truth* of God. We can only know God's will when we first know God's truth, for what God desires and requires of us must always be consistent with his character.[2]

Often churches have been built upon pain, bitterness, or pride to answer a human need.

Example of a Cracked Church Foundation

Early in the life of ministry that God has given me, I pastored my first church that was founded on being the only one in the community that had a decent Sunday school for children, even though others existed in the community. Although it is good to be proud of your Sunday school, it is not to be used to compare, contrast, and puff up your ministry. This kind of self-promoted exclusiveness can be a hindrance in ministry that petrifies a tunnel vision, limits a wider vision, and grows an internal corporate pride that is contrary to what a Christian church represents: Jesus Christ. Churches that have grown a "special" religious root of "being the best" at some ministry will have to pull it up later in an attitude of contrition and repentance.

Even with the superficial cover of programing and religion, this is a foundation that needs to be replaced by desires of God's heart and not our own. Only with his holy character can we see clearly through the horrors we tend to fixate on in a terribly sinful world.

---

2. Challies, *Discipline of Spiritual Discernment*, 54.

Why the Fatherless Lens?

Among the three repeated people groups throughout Scripture, the widow, the fatherless, and the stranger, none is timelier in giving us an exhortation from God as the reality of fatherlessness. The impact of fatherlessness is so devastating that we need to capture the principles of God's vision of ministry to this specific people group to make an impact upon this present world. Here are some current examples that illustrate the issue of fatherlessness.

First, almost all the social fabric of our society is affected by fatherlessness. Stephen Marche encapsulates the significant, far-reaching implications and impact of the fatherless.

> Fatherlessness as a condition has been linked with virtually every social ill you can name (the big exception being lesbian families): Young men who grow up without fathers are twice as likely to end up in jail, 63 percent of youths who commit suicide are from fatherless homes, and 71 percent of high school dropouts come from fatherless homes.[3]

God's instruction to us concerning this hurting group of people will show us the primary principles to measure and guide effective outreach in all areas of ministry.

Second, the power of fathering is the answer to fatherlessness. In aligning our sight with God's heart we see that fatherhood is crucially important. It is a foundational power to our society. Dr. Ken Canfield, the founder and president of the National Center for Fathering, said,

> A father has enormous power. About this, he has no choice. For good or for bad, by his presence or absence, action or inaction, whether abusive or nurturing, the fact remains: A father is one of the most powerful beings on the face of the earth.[4]

3. Marche, "Fatherhood Matters" 1–4.
4. Canfield, *Heart of a Father*, 17.

Fathering comes out of the nature of God; it is a power that has his expectation of proper stewardship and priority. The community of faith who trusts in a personal God must show it as a priority as well.

Third, the Word of God gives powerful guidance to combat the pain of "fatherlessness." The biblical context of how God sees "fatherlessness" is considered a primary source for spiritual discernment in outreach. Our study together will assume the person of God and his word as an ultimate authority in all aspects of spiritual vision, discernment, and family systems. A list of priorities emerges from our observations of God's view of the fatherless and his fatherly concerns. The series of priorities that come from God's focus on the fatherless are the following lenses (themes): Irreparable, Fatherhood, Trinity, Compassion, Authority, Relationship, Presence, Generational, Justice, and God-Worth (see figure 1). These themes are the largest points of the observed context surrounding the fatherless. They are revealed as most explicit by repeated emphasis, surrounding context, definition of words in context, connection to the word fatherless, connection to God's personhood, and connection with God's expectations and commands.

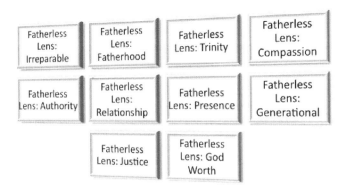

Figure 1. The Multifaceted Fatherless Lens That Reflects the Heart of God

A fourth reason for a focus on the fatherless as a way of looking at our local church ministry outreach is to see if we are specifically addressing the deep wounds of people rather than the superficial surface needs or issues.

> The fifth dirge of Lamentations indicates that one becomes an orphan solely through the loss of a father, even if the mother is still present. "We have become orphans and waifs, our mothers are like widows," (Lamentations 5:3). The *New American Standard Bible* reads, "We have become *orphans without a father*." The word orphan means, "to be lonely" and refers to a bereaved person. And bereaved people need to grieve both their tangible and intangible losses.[5]

A repeated theme from God is first introduced in Genesis 1:18, "It is not good for the man to be alone." Although the text is referring to a marriage relationship, the emphasis is on being alone. God commands us to bring into relationship those who are alone. The desolation of the fatherless is seen as unnatural and not a part of his creational intent. Being made in the image of God means that we are people made for relationship just as God is; it is reflected in the truth of the Trinity. God has made us for relationship. Tom Hanks in the movie *Castaway* vividly depicts what would happen if we were left alone for long amounts of time. We start developing a relationship with things like rocks, volleyballs, etc., and start talking to ourselves. We were created for a relationship with God. With God we are rejuvenated, and we are refreshed by those who reflect his image around us. God and others keep us from fantasy, madness, and delusions. In my role as a pastor and a chaplain, I have seen those who tear themselves down with words, practice self-mutilation, and repeatedly stop relationships because they have a fear of rejection; but the reality is that they have had no perceived relationship support system that would stick with them through hardship, grief, and also the good times. God expects us to reach out to those who are ebbing toward isolation, fetal positions, and even marring their own identity with abusive words and physical actions.

---

5. Robinson, *Longing for Daddy*, 51, emphasis added.

Finally, sin is powerful if one does not know the power of God through Jesus Christ. True brokenness brought about by selfish sinful mankind can be answered with the power of Jesus Christ lived out in us. The broken must intimately know the source of their healing and be convinced of the power of God that can be bestowed on them through our great Savior, Jesus Christ. Only when we properly grasp God as our Father are we ready to reach out to those around us who are of fatherless distress.

Are You Ready to Bring Wholeness to the Broken?

Without you, yourself, believing that *you* have the "power of God for salvation for those who believe," the broken will be left with no answers. The stories of helplessness are real and those who minister to the downtrodden are in the front lines of spiritual battle. If one is not equipped with the Word of God, personal knowledge of salvation through Jesus Christ, and a growing understanding of the heart of God, the result will be a spiritual battlefield casualty. Do not become just another good person with sincere temporary moralistic humanistic fixes. God addresses the deep separation between man and God. The destruction that sin brings is the fruit of not letting God insert his Son Jesus Christ into our lives.

Distress Is Everywhere

Once in a great while a haunting comes to the minister who counsels the helpless. If one is not spiritually alert it can catch him or her off guard. Satan loves to insert doubt into our lives when we use courage and initiative with God's Word. We also insert our own doubt into our lives when we set high expectations. The spiritual battlefield does not play out like a fairy tale. It is messy. Relationships overlap other relationships, ethical dilemmas, no quick fixes, tired investment of time and resources. We must be ready in season and out of season to give a powerful account of what God can do. The reason we as chaplains or ministers remember such times is that the crises gets replayed afterward and you wonder if you could have said something better or clearer. What a responsibility we have. But just like me, you also have this same responsibility. A woman the other day in a restaurant, which my wife and I were dining at, was crying very quietly for some time and was in obvious distress. I initiated an inquiry. Could I be of any help? Told her I was a minister and that my wife and I were ready and willing to listen to her concern. She politely said she was tired and had come off shift at a hospital and was phoning a family member to talk about whatever it was. We are reminded to visit the widow and orphan *in their distress*.[6] Most people in distress do not come into a minister's office somewhere from nine to five with an appointment. This means that you and I are on the front lines of the disillusioned every day.

One Distress Situation in the Military

A young woman came to me for counseling. Her situation was all too common and it was redundant in the sinful actions of many a relationship. She came from the streets; joined the US Army to make herself a better person and the family proud. Her great desire was to go into the big wide world and make bigger and better choices, changing a dictated and foreseeable destiny. She was committed to being different and not walking in the ways of her destructive siblings and the norms of the neighborhood. Nonetheless, her tears were many, she was pregnant, and the look, oh, the miserable expression. Wide and fearful eyes asking through the blur of tears, how!? How could this happen?

The fear almost took on a monstrous form dragging her into despair over and over again. Her culture and her core faith belief presented a determined map that was far different than she was experiencing. A bittersweet curve ball was thrown across her life. "I was determined, I was sincere, I believed," she said, and in her misery, she described, "I was on my way and somehow my

---

6. Jas 1:27.

past and circumstances grabbed me, took hold of me, and forced me back into the same cycles as my parents, siblings, and my neighborhood." It was her Christian way of cursing the situation, through gritted teeth, tears and great anger. Somehow she may have thought by coming to the chaplain, life could be reset like a computer. Sin would have its consequences that day, but as a servant of God, I was able to share with her the powerful word that God would be able to address the brokenness of her life.

Who is the person in your ministry that God is bringing to mind? Allow these principles to inform your involvement. So I ask, are you ready to address that which is close to the heart of God? Military power, environmental concerns, saving animals, finances and nutrition to name a few are of the temporal. Enter into the heart of God, understand his concerns, and accept his eternal priorities.

Leadership Study Questions

1. Read Psalm 10:14.

2. Discuss within your group who represents the "fatherless" in your local church ministry.

   Personalize Psalm 10:14 to your local ministry context: "But You, O God, do see trouble and grief; you consider it to take it in hand. The _____ commits himself to you; you are the helper of the _____."

3. The people you have identified, are they in your ministry plan? Are they represented on your missionary prayer board?

4. If the dominoes of "brokenness" were lined up in a row to fall in order (1–100), would the brokenness that you have identified in your community be the first domino?

5. What eternal powers are you addressing brokenness with? (Salvation / Restoration to God through Jesus Christ, the living Word of God; Prayer; Strong mentoring relationships; Testimonies of the saints; Followers of Jesus Christ in your midst; etc.?)

6. Pray to see the spiritual battlefield accurately (see Heb 4:13).

For Next Week

Read the next chapter.

- Read the "fatherless" passages.
- Pray to see as God sees your local church ministry.
- Gather local church ministry materials to be used in coming weeks (mission statement, vision statement, church phone answering machine message, ministry philosophy, etc.)

2

Irreparable

Do not take advantage of a widow or an orphan. If you do and they cry out to me, I will certainly hear their cry. My anger will be aroused, and I will kill you with the sword; your wives will become widows and your children fatherless.

—EXODUS 22:22–24

The King will reply, "I tell you the truth, whatever you did for one of the least of these brothers of mine, you did for me."

—MATTHEW 25:40

There are so many great causes and charities in the world and so many appeals for physical help, money, assets, and skill sets. Yet, God has set a priority in front of us much like one lays out a table setting in front of a guest. He has told us clearly about a need that cuts deep into his heart. Followers of God desire to know God's heart and trust his discernment of our brokenness. The days are evil and increasing in intensity with closer and closer birth pangs. Now is the time to steward what God has given us on the eternal.

As a people of God, should we not dwell upon the priority of brokenness that is always within his eyesight? For me, the answer is a resounding "Yes!"

The living church is God's instrument of outreach into our broken world. God has given us this repeated phrase, "fatherless," throughout Scripture to help us know what to focus upon. Let us explore the heart of God through this term "fatherless."

Commitment to the Irreparable

Consider this: can you restore a culture or country to the alien (stranger)? Can you bring a widow's husband back from the dead? Can you clean up a broken relationship between a child and his father who lives on the opposite side of the country? Can you bring a boy's dad back from the dead? Can you make up for lost time? Can you replace the arm or leg of an amputee? Can you, by yourself, forgive, restore, repent, and give the fullness of life back to a hurting person? Notice the forty-three "fatherless" Scripture passages point to the irreparable or "unfixable" people problems of our world. To openly address these problems is to encounter a brokenness that is beyond our ability to set right. Quite often we show our lack of faith by tackling the small fixable problems of the world that bring temporary circumstantial relief, but do nothing to advance the kingdom of God.

> Worship of ease is not a malady that affects individuals only. Churches also go to great lengths to avoid putting themselves in places where they may be uncomfortable. Churches are sometimes so concerned with their own glory, prestige, and comfort that they are tempted to direct their resources to ministries that will glorify their own kingdoms instead of Christ's.[1]

The church is God's instrument to reveal Jesus Christ living in us. The living church is called to do mighty deeds and take up that which the world chooses to ignore or not address because of

1. Bennett, *Passion for the Fatherless*, 125.

hopelessness. Efforts in a temporal world all look futile. The world does charity for the "now." Charity efforts of the world without Christ are truly humanistic, limited to this lifetime, and sacrifice is for the giver and not the brokenhearted.

A God walker, on the other hand, understands one's own brokenness and reaches out remembering the despair and destruction from which Jesus Christ saved them. Unfixable to the world is really and truly unfixable (using only human resources, wisdom, and effort), but to the saints of God who have been given power and authority to address the brokenness, the unfixable can be mended and the irreparable made like new. The living church addresses the unfixable with the almighty power of God. With God the irreparable is eternally repaired, the unfixable is eternally fixed, the broken hearted are healed and lifted up.

The outreach that God expects requires a great deal of dependence upon our powerful and present Father. This dependence upon God started when we admitted before God our brokenness and spelled out to him that our dark sin separated us from a Holy God. Dependence on God is called faith. The churches of Jesus Christ are the only people groups that can address the unfixable pain that has rippled through history. Unfixable situations, the irreparable, and destruction flow from when sin entered the world by our willful rebellion against God. Only saints declared holy can reach out with the eternal answers of a peace that passes all understanding, a joy unspeakable, and a grace undeserved that only comes through the blood sacrifice of Jesus Christ.

This is the confidence Christians share: With God nothing is "unfixable."[2] Sound familiar? By now, you should realize that the word "unfixable" is a way of showing the difference between the world and the Christian in addressing the deepest and most hurtful needs that have the attention of our Father God's heart.

2. Luke 1:37; Rom 8:37.

A Call to the Uncomfortable

Yes, the nursing home can be a smelly place. Yes, when I go to the hospital, I do not know what to say. Yes, that Sunday school class of boys is pure chaos. Yes, there are many uncomfortable places to show the love of Jesus Christ. But, that is where his love shines the brightest. In our brokenness, we are more than conquerors. We should go where the world as a whole does not want to go. We have real and eternal answers to those who are brokenhearted.

Look at your missionary board or list of ministries. Are there any ministries addressing messy, unfixable, hard, irreparable, or difficult situations? Are the saints of God in that church involved with the difficult or uncomfortable? A way of checking our determination to address the irreparable, is to see how much of our stewardship of time, talent, and money is applied into the "unfixable."

Missions are often left alone in a church body and administrated from afar. Look at how many times Paul was visited and supported by saints from the churches with money, visits, personal requests, and prayers. Ministry is not to be contracted out. What I mean by that is missions need to be more than a business arrangement. Missionaries are accountable to supporting churches and supporting churches are accountable to them. Has the missionary been visited to offer encouragement? Does the missionary have a need that could be supported by sweat and labor from those who pray for them diligently? The following story is a humorous way of making the point.

One time I met a soldier who was in hot water because for many years he told his wife that he was a "volunteer" reservist for the military. Most people know that when you are a part-time military reservist you get paid for your weekend and two weeks a year. The wife had not seen any of this money. Well, this soldier came to seek help because he had a lot of explaining to do. There was probably marriage counseling in his future as well. Likewise, how much do we know about our missionaries? Do we know enough to pray in some detail for them? Do we know enough to be specific in our support of what God has called them to do?

Concurrent giving is another way of looking at ministries. Compartmentalized efforts can keep us out of touch with ministry. Personally I pray better, give better, use my time better, and interact relationally better for a ministry I am involved in. Effort in prayer, time, talent, and money all need to be given together. Spiritual health comes to all who are giving and receiving. In this age of technology churches have been connecting to their missionaries across the globe right during the Sunday service. There is great connection power now days; we need to use it.

A long time ago and in a mission field not so far away, I was a teenager in a youth group in First Baptist Church of Medford, Oregon. Missionaries were a wonderment to me and more than a calling of God. Frankly, in my micro-vision they were odd—those who dropped everything and served a bunch of people that nobody gave much thought to in normal life.

The wise leadership of that church sanctioned a youth mission trip to work with a missionary that was supported by our congregation, in Northern California. Al was a missionary to migrant workers in the fields. In one week's time the collective energy of our youth group joined in ministry with our missionary. We played volleyball, we told Bible stories, we shared our testimonies, we made Bible backgrounds for flannel graph stories, prayed together and with the children we ministered to, and did fix-up and cleaning work. We also ate chocolate chip pancakes and cantaloupe every day. Conclusion: missionaries were no longer a far-off thought. Missionaries worked hard. Missionaries loved God by loving the people they gave their lives to. Missionaries needed support and specific prayers; not just, "Lord, bless the missionaries." Collectively, our youth group learned that missionaries live for the eternal, and sang as a truth, "this world is not my home, I am just passing through." The deep abiding, sacrificial and giving love of Al and his wife was poured out upon special people of God's creation that the rest of the world was willing to ignore.

Another example of awareness in reaching out to the hurting was seen in fifth and sixth graders who visited a nursing home next to the church. My wife, Karen, had the joy of teaching these actions of ministry, serving as Children's Christian Educator on staff. This included rolling them in (wheel chairs) to church, taking them back, caroling at Christmas, and bringing cookies on class visits. Investment: time, muscle, and cookie supplies. Result: wholeness and life abundant in the family of God. The lonely and ignored are addressed with the lens of fatherless.

"How long will this take?" is often our first thought when we encounter a need of any magnitude. Another way of testing our resolve to minister to the "unfixable" is in the area of time. What is the time commitment? Often we think in projects. A crusade, a revival, a vacation Bible school, a twelve-week Bible study is focused on, completed, and then we are ready for another project. Individuals are not to be thought of as projects. We often use the tools of investing in others' lives to insulate, separate, and distance ourselves from discomfort. It is even more ungodly if we are competing with other churches or ministries.

Equal giving in time, talent, and money brings with it a building up of the saints of God and awareness. Ministry is an "all-in" commitment.

All churches are called to practice true and undefiled religion by reaching out to the "fatherless" or the disenfranchised within their "distress."[3] Each church needs to weigh the mission to the community around them to show how important the lens is to their church according to what God has given them to steward.[4] Such things as physical location (inner city or urban), people groups (ethnic, gender, etc.), specific brokenness (drugs, alcohol, domestic, specific kind of crime, etc.), and resources available can be considered.

3. Jas 1:27.
4. The Great Commission.

A Positive Personal Promise when You Reach Out to the Helpless

James 1:27 says that when we reach out to the widow and orphan in their distress, we are able "to keep [ourselves] from being polluted by the world." Basically, when you wade into the muck of life as God defines it, the promise of this specific obedience is authentication of mission and clarity of address. Bottom line, the world will have less influence on you. Like a teenager who goes on a mission trip and opens themselves up to greater giving, they come back less enabled to be fooled by the world and its self-delusion. Even better, you see a miracle. Like a crystal glass that has been shattered to pieces, there is no one in the world that can put it back together again just like it was, except God the Creator. When you enter into the brokenness of the world with God's power, you will see the miracle of his healing possible "on earth as it is in heaven."[5] The temporal will become dim and the eternal will become clearer. You will have a greater immunity to the world's influences.

5. Matt 6:10.

Leadership Study Questions

1. Have we reached out to the most broken in our area of influence? Do we believe we have been given power to do it? (See Matt 17:20–21.)

2. Who are the people represented by the widow and orphan in our church and community?

   (See Exodus 22:22–24.)

   "The King will reply, 'I tell you the truth, whatever you did for one of the _____ of these brothers of mine, you did for me'" (Matt 25:40).

3. Do we reach out as broken people saved by the blood of Jesus Christ or do we reach out from an impression of perfection?

4. Are we comfortable in our outreach ministry? Have we tried the uncomfortable?

5. Does our support for ministry outreach include our physical involvement? Is outreach ministry distant from us?

6. Is there parallel giving (of time, talents, and resources) in most areas of our outreach ministry?

7. Who are the "least of these brothers of mine?" (See Matt 25:40.)

8. What will be the result of practicing true and undefiled religion according to James 1:27?

For Next Week

Read the next chapter.

- Read the "fatherless" passages.
- Pray to see the "unfixable" in your local church ministry.

- Identify your church's purposefulness in reaching the broken, downtrodden, or irreparable people groups of your area.

3

Fatherhood

A father to the fatherless, a defender of widows, is God in his holy dwelling.

—PSALM 68:5

I will be a Father to you, and you will be my sons and daughters, says the LORD Almighty.

—2 CORINTHIANS 6:18

Fatherhood is God's norm for his kingdom, so when God addresses the "fatherless," it ought to cause us to pay attention. Since God emphasizes in forty-three Scripture passages that there is a lack of a father, it shows repeatedly that he hates this part of the destructive nature of sin. Because God relates to us as a father, many from broken backgrounds have a hard time seeing the character of God as a loving father. In our broken world our community has chosen an abnormal way of life that gives us a weaker foundation of presenting God the Father.

An absent father doesn't provide security for the child, nor can that absent father consistently and appropriately discipline. The fatherless child may come to the conclusion that since survival thus far hasn't included a father, survival in the future does not necessitate God the Father.[1]

Ministry in the local church must demonstrate God as our Father so that further unfolding of his person can heal the wounds of the downcast.

Fatherhood Is God's Choice Way of Relating to Us

An observation of God's compassionate heart is that he has chosen to relate to us as a father.[2] That simple undeniable fact throughout Scripture needs to be included as one of our lenses in "fatherless" outreach ministry. Fatherhood is countercultural in today's world. God expects intentional fatherhood. John Eldredge states the personal fact and vision of God in regard to fathering.

We aren't meant to figure life out on our own. God wants to father us. The truth is, he *has* been fathering us for a long time—we just haven't had the eyes to see it. He wants to father us much more intimately, but we have to be in a posture to receive it. What that involves is a new way of seeing, a fundamental reorientation of how we look at life, and our situation in it.[3]

While many are used to relating to God as our Father, it is unfortunate that there are many who because of their broken frame of reference have a hard time understanding God as "Father." For our study, we will go beyond the dynamic of our own personal relationship with Father God and try to see fatherhood as God wants it displayed in ministry outreach. God the Father chooses to father us in relationship, and this begs the question, should

1. Tolbert, "Relationship," 200.
2. Ps 68:5; Luke 2:49.
3. Eldredge, *Fathered by God*, 11.

we chose to father the helpless in our ministry area of influence? God's role as a father to us is foundational in understanding God's mind and heart. The word "father" represents initiation, identity, love, strength, and direction beyond simply contributing to the birth of a child. A child without a father will search the rest of their life looking for those very items. People want to know where they came from and how they got here. It is a normal question. People want to be informed about their identity; not just for physical health reasons, but for knowing how they fit into their family and community as a whole. It is a start, a handle, a foundation, to progress in life. Each person wants to know about the love that brought them into this world. Each person holds valuable the people who raised them from innocent ignorance to a functioning form of adult life. A person wants to know about the sustaining strength of their heritage to live up to. People desire to find a moral fiber in their heritage because God has set eternity in their heart and it is a reflection of God the Father. How did I start? What should my direction be?

In a child's physical development they learn to be independent. First they roll over, then scoot, crawl, waddle, walk, and reach for toys, etc. Children are helped by strong, loving hands and arms. Encouraging words and exclamations are expressed. Food, sleep, protection, and time are provided for by a mom and a dad. In general, the mom gives the child the strength of nurturing; it is deep, life sustaining, and follows the child into adulthood. In general, the dad gives the strength of empowerment; it is deep, life sustaining, and follows the child into adulthood. Each role is equally important to God. God made it this way and he knows what is best for his creation. Spend your time "bucking it," you move toward the chaos and destruction of a family. In today's terminology, anything different is a dysfunctional lifestyle that does not represent the fullness of life that God wants us to have. Praise God for the single parents who recognize their lack and work hard to put an ambassador of motherhood or fatherhood into a child's life.

Presently I teach thirty-six juvenile boys from seventh grade to eleventh grade in a residential boys' home. A majority are there because of the lack of a father. Can they be successful in life? Yes, but God created us for a relationship with a father. My dad did not have one for most of his life, yet by the grace of God, he fathered six children to maturity. God has promised to step in and father the fatherless.

Fatherhood: A Preserving Salt in Society

Fatherhood is often minimized by society. Turn on your TV and you will in short time see in commercials and shows the bumbling dad trying to father. Yet, fatherhood is crucial to the fabric of societal strength. In the past a father was seen as an asset to the community; a person of authority in their own home, but had an extended influence in the community. God our Creator is a Father to us individually and as a people who look to him collectively. There are repeated references to "the children of Israel" and God being a collective "father to the fatherless." Part of God's exhortation concerning the fatherless is that we have a community responsibility. We are valuing individualism and compartmentalization over community and family. The value of fatherhood extends past the family and the individual father given to us by God. Society as a whole benefits from a multitude of responsible fathers who take their role seriously. Leading and being responsible for your own family is just the beginning of a father's influence in the world. David Blankenhorn, founder and president of the Institute for American Values, informs us of the strength of fatherhood in society:

> Fatherhood is a social role that obligates men to their
> biological offspring. For two reasons, it is society's most
> important role for men. First, fatherhood, more than

any other male activity, helps men to become good men: more likely to obey the law, to be good citizens, and to think about the needs of others. Put more abstractly, fatherhood bends maleness—in particular, male aggression—toward prosocial purposes. Second, fatherhood privileges children. In this respect, fatherhood is a social invention designed to supplement maternal investment in children with paternal investment in children.[4]

David Blankenhorn breaks down the paternal investment of fatherhood as follows:

Paternal investment enriches children in four ways. First, it provides them with their father's physical protection. Second, it provides them with a father's money and other material resources. Third, and probably the most important, it provides them with what might be termed paternal cultural transmission: a father's distinctive capacity to contribute to the identity, character, and competence of his children. Fourth, and most obviously, paternal investment provides children with the day-to-day nurturing—feeding them, playing with them, telling them a story—that they want and need from both of their parents.[5]

The lengthy quote clearly states the many strong purposes of the importance of the role of fatherhood. God the Creator simply states the importance by the implication of the word "fatherless." In our ministry, do we elevate the importance of fatherhood or have our churches become empty shells echoing the falsehoods and forms of godliness that our society dictates to us? Outreach to the disenfranchised needs to have the powerful strength of fatherhood. There is a longing for its strength whether in the anger of lack or the frustration of a broken family.

The pastoral advice of Dr. Kent Hughes reminds us of the power of fatherhood.

---

4. Blankenhorn, *Fatherless America*, 25.
5. Ibid., 25.

Men, as fathers you have such power! You will have this terrible power till you die, like it or not—in your attitude toward authority, in your attitude toward women, in your regard for God and the Church. What terrifying responsibilities! This is truly the power of life and death.[6]

Again, we are looking at God's vision of the fatherless and how that instructs our local church ministry. Although there are other biblical metaphors of God revealed to us, God sees ministry with a fatherhood angle. He has placed his Son, Jesus Christ, as head of the church. God has approved Jesus Christ as the doorway to redemption. Fatherhood is central to our everyday relationship with God. Does our local church ministry include the aspect of fatherhood? If we are to have a ministry that is based upon the principles of fatherhood, then it also should be comfortable with masculinity. Present day exhorters like John Eldredge are raising a voice to be unapologetic concerning manhood. There are some strong masculine characteristics of God that are unused in many churches and ministry outreach can suffer for it. Sports, muscles, outdoors, and adventure are just as important as teas, coffees, and potlucks. It is the nature of God to always win (because he is God), to bring us to the edge of life to teach us a lesson, and to take on responsibility in the joy of fatherhood. There are affirmations and "rites of passage" that boys and men are in need of.

> All masculine initiation is ultimately spiritual. The tests and challenges, the joys and adventures are all designed to awaken a man's soul, draw him into contact with the masculine in himself, in other men, in the world, and in God, as Father.[7]

In one word, fatherhood, God emphasizes the importance of both masculinity and fathering. God's challenge regarding the "fatherless" is not cultural and it is not sexist, it is a revelation as to how God wants us to proceed as a holy people to reach out to

---

6. Hughes, *Disciplines*, 47.

7. Eldredge, *Fathered by God*, 209.

a spiritually dark world. Is there space in our ministry area for manhood?

Space for Fatherhood

My father, who should not have succeeded at fatherhood except for the power of God in his life, had space for manhood. As a pastor, shepherd, and preacher of the highest order in my eyes, he loved God's people. In modern thinking, he started life with several disadvantages . . . no dad at age eight, a mother in a mental institution, never staying in a school for more than a half year and on his own at an early age. The world has no answers for such brokenness. For all the heaviness of life he could have focused on, he chose joy. In my adult years, I have come to realize that first and foremost, his joy was rooted in his Savior, Jesus Christ. The second source of joy was being married to my mom and being a father to six children who experienced what he never had.

With a son on both ends of four girls, camping was our economical family vacation of choice. Activities we enjoyed were fishing trips and men's retreats common in the Northwest. Depending on the church, he would steer his six-member tribe into Boys Club, King's Sons or King's Daughters back before AWANA became popular. He brought us along to men's prayer breakfasts. He encouraged us to be involved in the youth groups and Sunday school, always taking a special interest in what we were learning. Reflecting back, the church body ministered to my dad by modeling other father-son relationships. He pastored a church, but depended upon men being spiritual examples of leading and being responsible stewards of their families and church body. A service he always put great time and effort into was the Lord's Supper. All the elected spiritual leadership of the church sat in the front and served the congregation. These were men who were not afraid to kneel in prayer. These were men who were willing to shoulder and prioritize family, church, and work responsibilities. These were men who would quietly work in the background of the church doing a multitude of ministry activities that would meet the needs of the saints without seeking any fanfare. It was always understood that the special "benevolent" offering only taken at this service would be distributed by the discerning men of the church and applied to the needs of our own congregation. Fervent in their prayers, duties, and protection of the saints of God, our church was safe and strong. The communion service always had a special family feel to it. This is what I mean when I say, a 'space for fatherhood."

Helping Fill the Gap

Most of the time on military retreats we cater to the adventurous young single male and challenge them to go canoeing or repelling, to play paintball, or to engage some other challenge. As an Army chaplain, I remember pushing this one single mom to bring her son on a kayaking trip off the coast of Georgia. At the time, I thought I was addressing the spiritual needs of the fifteen soldiers who went on this trip. Indeed that was happening, but God used the trip to open my eyes to the needs of single-parent soldiers. As a result of that trip with this particular soldier/mom and her son, their bond grew stronger. The boy did not stop talking about that trip for a very long time. Later, the mom confessed to me that she may not have done such an adventurous thing with her son unless I had gently pushed her into the retreat. This is the "fatherhood" dynamic that needs to be repeated in the body of Christ. Fatherhood and motherhood are to influence the community at large.

Let Us Not Water It Down

In this world's value on words of "inclusiveness" and "accommodation," do we have space in our fellowships for fatherhood, motherhood, and the celebration of children? We are not representing God favorably if we think spirituality is blending distinct roles together to the point of meaninglessness. There are broken people who do not know what a father looks like. There are searching people who have not experienced a mother. There are devastated people who have not seen a family as God has set it up. There is a longing for a whole family without knowing why. Broken people gravitate to, yet cautiously approach, a strength that may heal their wounds. Fatherhood for all time will represent that strength. It is the godly strength that God expects to be applied to the wounds of the downtrodden!

Leadership Study Questions

1. Have we provided a "fatherhood" representation of God in our worship and outreach?

   "I will be a _____ to you, and you will be my sons and daughters, says the LORD Almighty" (2 Cor 6:18).

2. Does our worship reflect a balance of both the nurture and power of God?

3. What kind of brokenness is addressed by fatherhood? (See Ps 68:5.)

4. Do we have programs and methods that help strengthen the fathers of the church and our view of God as a Father?

5. Do we have a testimony of strength in our church that represents God the Father?

6. Is the strength of family represented in our congregation? (See 2 Cor 6:18.)

For Next Week

Read the next chapter.

- Read the "fatherless" passages.
- Pray for fatherhood to be seen in your local church ministry.
- Identify your church's celebration of fatherhood, motherhood, and children.

4

Trinity

The LORD watches over the alien and sustains the fatherless and the
widow, but he frustrates the ways of the wicked.

—PSALM 146:9

May the grace of the Lord Jesus Christ, and the love of God, and the
fellowship of the Holy Spirit be with you all.

—2 CORINTHIANS 13:14

The Divine Triad—What Does It Tell Us?

A further observation of the "widow, orphan, and alien," found
in most of the Pentateuch, forms a "trinitarian" phrase, expressing the need of compassion in a complete community. God chose
the extremely helpless, the weakest, the alienated, the needy, and
the most likely to be marginalized by a holy people to be a three-
part exhortation of outreach. This outreach predates the more
familiar great commission in Matthew and gives us insight that

the Godhead has been intently focused on restoration through-out the ages. God chose Israel to be a holy people, set apart to be miniature examples or mirror images of God's just, merciful and restorative hand from the land and bondage of Egypt. As such, God commanded his people to bring the "aloneness" among them into "wholeness" or a connected relationship.

In the absolute eternal God, we have the doctrine of the Trinity. It is important to point out the Trinitarian relationship of God; it is an unmistakable truth that he jealously protects right relationships because by his very nature he is a relational being. This gives us insight to the non-relational bent of sin. One reason sin is destructive is because of its alienation of others in pursuit of selfish ends. Within the paradigm of religion, the selfish nature of man often limits one's sight to avoid an investment that is uncom-fortable. Our limitation of sight can also be caused by our passion to restore one aspect of the hurting person, blinding us to other needs. An example would be a person who has a passion to see the justice of God the Father meted out and in the process ignores mercy. Another example may be someone who greatly desires the unconditional compassion of Jesus, but while their interpretation of Christ's love is being poured out, it may be done so without ad-dressing a person's worth or dignity. Trinitarian sight sees with the depth of relationship. When Jesus healed the woman with the "is-sue of blood," he went to great lengths to not only heal, but to bring her back into community, and even more so, to replace and restore a relationship of fear and shame to one of confidence and human dignity.[1] Where she felt isolation from everyone at multiple levels before, she was restored. Jesus touched the leper.[2] Leprosy brought loneliness and a lack connectedness to the community. Sin and its effects afflict people in this way. The leper was connected back to the community through a proclamation of "cleanness" from the priests. Jesus restored intimately one on one and then with family, and community. Jesus was not afraid to show God's power when

1. Matt 9:20–22; Mark 5:25–34, note: same story—great phrase added, "Go in peace and be freed from your suffering."

2. Matt 8:2–4.

needed, but also was not afraid to show the intimacy of a loving God.

Many times I have met believers who reflect the intimacy of Christ by introducing and connecting someone in a wheel chair, a disabled veteran, or a Down syndrome individual, with others in the community of faith. Sometimes unfortunately we also still have to connect when there are perceived or real cultural, ethnic, or gender hurdles. The intimacy of the Trinity does not allow us to leave anyone out. We must extinguish aloneness and connect all relationships into community. Churches seem to be hot or cold on connectedness. Some churches "dog pile" on the personal introduction, connection, the good news of the gospel, and your possible future involvement in their local church in the first five minutes of walking in the door (this might be a bit much). But some churches are like a stone-cold tomb. You can slip in and out of them without anybody knowing your name, that you came, and that you exist. I present both extremes, so that saints of God may have a plan to connect with people in and out of a Sunday church service.

God chooses to express himself in a triune presentation in reaching out to the disenfranchised. Dr. Randy Woodley also observes this in relationship to the concept of God's priority of shalom.

> The *disempowered triad* of widows, orphans, and strangers best represents God's concern for those who have few material goods (food, clothing, shelter) and who are most easily oppressed (justice). Shalom addresses God's concern for the socially marginalized.[3]

Dr. Woodley further observed that this triad was to be a part of a holy people's thinking and further explains its worldwide implications:

> God's intention was that Israel use their unfortunate circumstances, the time of slavery in Egypt when they had nothing, to check their attitude toward the poor

3. Woodley, *Shalom*, 16.

and marginalized. The Creator's concern for shalom communities to be built on justice and care for the poor went past Israel and stretched to all the boundaries of the earth.[4]

Dr. Woodley has observed this repeated formula as a major platform or theology to extend our hand to the broken. It is our "reasonable," "rational," "spiritual" service of worship.[5]

Biblical Triads

Throughout Scripture God chooses to express his heart in triads. The three-part revelation often correlates to the nature of each person of the Godhead. If brought to an ultimate congruent conclusion, then we, if made in the image of God, have a vested interest in this expression. "Love the LORD your God with all your heart and with all your soul and with all your strength"[6] along with "to act justly and to love mercy and to walk humbly with your God,"[7] are triad actions in a community that reaches out in reflection of the person and nature of a triune God, "the Father, the Son, and the Holy Spirit."[8] A defending Father, a loving Jesus, a comforting Holy Spirit reaching out to brokenness is the nature of the loving reach of a personal God. God's line of sight into our broken world is triune. We are to reach out and reveal God to a broken world in triune ways. A holy people reach out to more than one dimension of a person. Dr. Erickson emphasizes:

> Furthermore, the perfect love and unity within the Godhead model for us the oneness and affection that should characterize our relationships within the body of Christ.[9]

4. Ibid., 17.
5. Rom 12:1–2.
6. Deut 6:5.
7. Mic 6:8.
8. 2 Cor 13:14.
9. Erickson, *Introducing Christian Doctrine*, 115.

God has directed us "to be conformed to the likeness of his Son."[10] If we are conforming to Jesus, then we are learning Christianity 101.

Perceiving with Depth

A triune vision brings about a vision of depth in our outreach to the "fatherless, widows, and the alien." As much as we would like to be masters at outreach we cannot see everything. We need to have depth in meeting needs. We need to have depth in providing multiple relationships. We need to have depth in not only fixing something, but tracing the pain or lack back to the first cause and address that issue as well. Hunger can be solved in the here and now, but where did it come from and what supportive relationships are lacking? Is it knowledge of agriculture, employment, water system, or a way of supplying food that is really the need? A spouse has lost a loved one; we listen, we council, we bury, we grieve. Beyond the food provided for the week following is a need of supportive relationships; not replacing the spouse but learning through the support of others how to go on. Not just survive, but how to live in God's grace and power. God shows us three ways or examples of how to look at needs, and challenges and informs his church on multiple levels, with the triune phrase "widow, orphan, and alien." Age, gender, ethnicity, lack of family, lack of physical and emotional support, lack of self-determination, defenselessness, lack of future or vision, need that requires others, food, money, belonging, and address of generational damage are (not limited to) the many items that can be seen in God's early triad. Comparison of need is often not beneficial nor does it increase or decrease the fact that need exists. But comparison of three societal plights that open our eyes to need is beneficial in challenging a holy people, who have salvation in their remembrance, to what "real" need is. Through this divine triad vision, God is informing us of the breadth and width of brokenness that exists because of sin, and how to bring about his kingdom. The

---

10. Rom 8:29.

triune vision of God calls a local church to not only perceive brokenness, but to act and pursue with depth. Again, we must see with a
depth in time, space, relationships, and causality of the obvious need
in front of us. Dr. Peter Penner, director of Contextual Missiology,
explains our mission this way:

> The missional Church—the whole Church in mis-
> sion—has a triune mission, which is not limited to soul
> winning, as it is still sometimes understood. The mis-
> sional Church must . . . humbly fulfill the mission that all
> creation is already doing, that is, worship the Triune in
> words and deeds. It is through this triune mission—the
> same mission for which Jesus was sent—that the Church
> participates in the wider mission of God.[11]

The emphasis by Dr. Penner is a needed reminder to balance
our outreach to the world; the gospel is presented by word, action, teaching, modeling, witness, etc. We present the gospel in
depth and worship of God. Our actions toward the downcast are
expressions of the gospel. Jesus empowered us to go into the entire
world. How?[12] How often have we seen white churches ignore the
Hispanic / Indian / African American cultures (to name a few) in
our own backyard? Local churches move away from God's mission, become stagnant or dying and their light is removed from
them.[13] For these dying churches, the reach of God has essentially
become a withered arm.

It Is Not about Us, It's about God

Is our commitment to ministry of such great depth that it does not
have to be about our idea, program, or ego, or thrust? It is Jesus
Christ's church and he can manage it however he chooses.[14] The
following is an example of seeing with depth.

11. Penner, "Discerning and Following," 36–37.
12. Matt 28:18–20; Acts 1:7–8.
13. Rev 2:5.
14. Mark 9:38–41; Rom 8:31.

As a military chaplain it was my joy to work with Child Evangelism Fellowship Military Children's Ministry to open up "Good News" clubs on our local military installation. Although it is a goal to minister to military children specifically, along the journey of challenging local churches to provide teachers, prayer and continuity for the public schools in the military area of influence, other victories have occurred. As we visit churches asking them to consider our challenge for outreach, the scales from their eyes fall off and they see a public school across the street from their own church. When these churches consider helping the military or reaching out to their local public schools, they rightly choose to open a Bible Club in the public school next door to their facility. In the world of numbers, comparison, and completion one would say that the military lost and the local church won in ministry effort. In the process of sharing the military children's ministry with local churches, one must be willing for God to work in hearts and lives to the detriment of our own personal ministry goals. When a body of believers decides to move forward together toward God's purposes (fatherless principles) in obedience, the actions of ego (competition, comparing, and clamoring for attention) melt away.

The Small Church Influence Is Not Small

A similar situation occurs, especially in small churches when the saints have prayed for, taught, modeled, loved, supported a young person in the name of Jesus Christ. Even though the small struggling church would like to keep him or her there, they recognize the hand of God on their life and let them go to a lifetime of ministry elsewhere. Frankly, my mortal mind does not understand these things, but I have seen enough to know that Jesus Christ is in charge of his church and he works in it for eternal purposes. My heart goes out to churches that often experience this. Although my home church does not struggle in the area of personnel, it is still my home church. It is made up of saints who poured themselves out as a drink offering so that I could be an Army chaplain for over twenty-five years. They loved, supported, encouraged, taught, prayed, reminded, shepherded, modeled, and sent me out with their blessings. All of it was done selflessly without expectation of return. No matter the size of a church or program, influence in God's program is still only gained one person at a time. The big splashes of exciting ministry are made up of individual saints proclaiming the good news in a clear way to one person who needs God.

A Word of Encouragement

Let me encourage those who have sent their spirit-filled saints into the harvest fields; you have seen with depth. When a pastor, missionary, evangelist, or teacher is doing the "work of the ministry" because of your selfless sending, each decision for Christ, each counseling session, each sitting with the grief stricken, and each shepherding act moving people toward the fullness of life in Jesus Christ is in no small part *you* in them. You are moving with Trinitarian unity and practicing the fatherless principles.

It is Jesus Christ's church and he can manage it however he chooses.[15] Regardless of our ignorance of the "way" God moves in the priorities of the kingdom of God, his saints can trust his guidance and be guaranteed of their divine direction. The end result: God is glorified and faithful effective outreach is accomplished.

Older saints of God who have influenced me often have perceived me with depth. Their questions and comments often slice through to the bottom line or the "real" issue. This kind of depth only comes from faithfully walking with God and prayerfully looking at people with his eyes. A God who sees in such a triune way calls us to envision outreach from multiple directions, depth of need, unity in purpose, and a great dependence on his eyesight. Our theology and paradigm of outreach, then, is to include a trinitarian depth.

15. Mark 9:38–41; Rom 8:31.

Leadership Study Questions

1. Do we have a three-deep approach to local church outreach? (E.g., *Evangelism*: a. presentation of the gospel, b. discipleship, c. spiritual ministry or leadership; *Missions*: a. mission financial support, b. mission trip to encourage / pray / affirm / build up / discern further needs to be met, c. additional leadership or support as a result of involvement with local church missionary; *Benevolent Fund: a. food, gas, and money,* b. respect / prayer / visiting to meet further needs, c. providing means for extra income or provision/independence/ dignity.)

2. Does our church have a story about God moving willing ministry participants a different direction?

3. Is the unity in our congregation reflective of the Trinity?

   "May the _____ of the Lord Jesus Christ, and the _____ of God, and the _____ of the Holy Spirit be with you all" (2 Cor 13:14).

4. Share your favorite triad in Scripture (e.g., Deut 6:4–5; Mic 6:8; 2 Cor 13:14).

5. Is there a depth of spiritual sight in our ministry goals?

6. Do we minister with old ideas? Do we have some "original" ideas that reflect a reach into our unique community?

7. Do we reevaluate the "fatherless" landscape around our church?

For Next Week

Read the next chapter.

- Read the "fatherless" passages.
- Pray for the unity and depth of the Trinity to be seen in your local church ministry.

- Identify your church's teaching of the Trinity. Can your congregation identify in Scripture where the teaching of the Trinity is? (E.g., Matt 3:13–17; Matt 28:18–20; Acts 1:7–8; 2 Cor 13:14)

5

Compassion

This is what the LORD Almighty says: "Administer true justice; show mercy and compassion to one another. Do not oppress the widow or the fatherless, the alien or the poor. In your hearts do not think evil of each other."

—ZECHARIAH 7:9–10

For he says to Moses, "I will have mercy on whom I have mercy, and I will have compassion on whom I have compassion." It does not, therefore, depend on man's desire or effort, but on God's mercy.

—ROMANS 9:15–16

Compassion: What Is It?

Another word that needs greater fidelity in "fatherless" outreach is compassion. God sees with "racham": compassion. The word compassion is also interchanged at times with mercy in the Old

Testament.[1] Within the forty-three "fatherless" references, the word compassion is mentioned sparingly but implied mightily with the actions God expects from his people; furthermore, it can be exercised with all the "fatherless" lenses that we are exploring in this study.[2] Compassion, mercy, and encouragement are "soft" and nurturing words. Compassion, mercy, and encouragement are needed from surrogate fathers to bridge the gap. One finds in worship settings that compassion and mercy are ideals that are greatly talked, sung, and thought about but are not often acted upon with a great deal of intention. These words are often implied in church mission, vision, and philosophy of ministry statements, but the reality (temperature) needs to be checked often.

As noted previously, we as created, limited human beings tend to focus microscopically on the part of compassion that comes from our own limited experience. We focus too narrowly on a portion of compassion. Mothers Against Drunk Driving (MADD)[3] started with the loss of life and a strong sense that justice should prevail. Food banks and pantries show a tremendous amount of mercy and compassion over and over again, but in and of themselves do not move individuals toward a self-worth that solves a greater portion of the problem. Robert Lupton has said, "Compassion beckons us into unexplored territory."[4] He further explained God's balance in exercising compassion:

> Mercy is a force that compels us to acts of compassion. But in time mercy will collide with an ominous, opposing force. Injustice. Against this dark and overpowering force, acts of mercy can seem meager. What good is a sandwich and a cup of soup when a severe addiction has control of a man's life? Or a night in a shelter for a young woman who must sell her body to feed her child?

---

1. Hos 14:3; Zech 7:9–10.

2. Zech 7:9–10 is in the context of both mercy and compassion.

3. See the Mothers Against Drunk Driving website, http://www.madd.org.

4. Lupton, *Toxic Charity*, 40–41.

Perhaps that is why the Bible places equal emphasis on both mercy and justice. The ancient prophet Micah succinctly summarizes God's design: "He has shown you, O mortal, what is good. And what does the LORD require of you? To act justly and to love mercy and to walk humbly with your God" (6:8, NIV).[5]

Ministry and outreach has the element of mercy. Robert Lupton emphasizes rightly, "Mercy is also the portal through which we glimpse the heart of God."[6] God sees his creation through eyes of mercy.[7] The heart of God sees with mercy and compassion and balances it with justice.[8] It is a part of who God is. The church's outreach is to be merciful so that the world will question its sanity; fight so hard for justice that the world will stand aghast at its authoritative God-driven determination.

Context of Compassion

Compassion needs to be further defined in context because it is often only understood according to our own self-definition. Because of humanity's great brokenness, we often lose its meaning in our good intentions and do not follow the compassionate heart of God. Daniel Bennett, a pastor who equips the local church to care for orphans, describes this in a pithy way.

> The problem with passionless compassion is that it sees the means—compassion—as an end. It focuses on good deeds without first focusing on the worship that should motivate the believer to engage in them. Compassion is a means to an end and not the end itself.[9]

---

5. Ibid., 40–41.

6. Ibid., 42.

7. Eph 2:4.

8. According to *Strong's Concordance*, compassion and mercy cross over each other in meaning.

9. Bennett, *Passion for the Fatherless*, 48.

In our human aching hearts of mercy we often forget the aspect of God's will in showing compassion.[10] Compassion is not an end unto itself. "I will cause all my goodness to pass in front of you, and I will proclaim my name, the LORD, in your presence. I will have mercy on whom I will have mercy, and I will have compassion on whom I will have compassion."[11] God's compassion comes out of choice, not feeling. It is not accidental, not circumstantial, and not because of another's conviction of the mission. While we were a depraved mess, God chose to love us.[12] His compassion comes from who he is; his person. Likewise, we are to choose to show compassion based upon the character of God infused into our life because God chose to show us his great mercy.[13] Compassion is a part of the heart and head of God. Our exercise of this exact value brings glory to him. Compassion is partly an act of the will and partly knowing the priorities of the heart of God. Our compassion is based on God's will in reaching out to us.[14]

My ministry presently is to teach thirty-six juvenile boys in a residential camp facility. Many come in angry at their family, the system, courts, themselves, and anyone else that comes near them. When they are introduced into a new setting they often share their wrath with the person who is trying to help them. You see, others have tried to help them before and those individuals, in the boys' eyes, let them down. After they have tested you with their cursing, and unchecked emotion, they settle down. Our team is mature and is in it for the long haul. This is one of the most important characteristics they can see in our compassion. Compassion must be joined with a decision of the will when we reflect it God's way.

10. Rom 9:15.
11. Exod 33:19.
12. Rom 5:8.
13. 1 Pet 1:3.
14. Exod 22:21; 23:9; Rom 5:8.

Compassion Is When You Would Do It Over Again

One dark night when I was a teenager my dad, a pastor, was about to hand me a teachable moment. He got a call late at night from a man who needed some money for gas and food. Dad knew the hour was inopportune and unsafe so he had me wait in the car as he met the man in the park at dusk. Back then, ten dollars was like twenty presently. All went well and the man took the money and my dad came back to the car. But instead of going home we "staked the park out" to see what the man would do. Dad had been in the Army and had gut instinct for what people might or might not do. Yet, that did not stop him from doing what he believed the Lord would have him do. Sure enough, after a short amount of time, the man walked across the street for cigarettes and what we could only assume was alcohol. We had a great conversation after that concerning giving. The short of it is, Dad would do the same thing again, but if asked by that same man, he being a responsible steward would say, "No, I cannot help you today."

The conflict between godly compassion to the fatherless and pragmatic compassion (when it suits my feelings) is solved with comprehension of Romans 5:8b: "While we were still sinners, Christ died for us." As a military chaplain, I often paraphrased it for my soldiers, "While we were still face down in our vomit." Graphic, I know—but this can illustrate and magnify God's love, willed for us despite our filthy mess. This is why we show compassion, because God loved us in our mess, unconditionally, knowing that there would be those who choose him and those that would not. Likewise, we are to reach out without expectation of return, "the salvation prayer," or a "thank you." We choose to reach out in compassion, because God chose to reach out in compassion to us. This is his heart, this is the nature of his being, and this is who we ought to be.

Compassion Is a Part of Outreach

Not only is the beginning of wisdom to fear God: but God will show compassion upon those who fear him.[15] As we revere God we are promised both wisdom and compassion. Those who know God as their father will be inclined toward compassion and wisdom. Strong's Concordance defines the Hebrew: to love, have compassion, which is a verb. Our local church ministries are to embed compassion into their outreach. Dr. Penner, president and director of contextual missiology at International Baptist Theological Seminary of the European Baptist Federation, Prague, Czech Republic, comments on the importance of compassion:

> I would suggest that instead of the two terms, "liberation and power," the Church should use a term that witnesses to the motives of Christ and should be ours as well: compassion. Luther looked for this grace, mercy, and love; and this is what the world needs today—people desperately need to experience this compassion and belonging. Our mission should reflect God's way of mission in this world, our discerning and following the missionary God, and liberating all for the reign of God.[16]

A father's compassion is a mirror of God's compassion. In our outreach framework we need to include the exercise of a willful compassion, not an aching heart compassion that makes us feel good.

Compassion, mercy, and encouragement are liberally stated "buzzwords" with unattached actions of outreach. These words must be fleshed out in the local church. The words of compassion must have a plan, mission, and a purpose that reflects our Father God.

Encouragement is an outreach that God expects us to be a participant in.[17] Encouragement, in Hebrew, is a verb that means to be established. In the Common Greek of the New Testament,

---

15. Prov 1:7; 15:33; Ps 103:13.
16. Penner, "Discerning and Following," 39.
17. Ps 10:17–18.

encouragement more directly speaks of exhortation or charging another with truth.[18] It means to call to or for, to exhort, to encourage. It is a verb with the corresponding words of encourage, console, summon, entreat, admonish, comfort.[19] Encouragement contains that which is true, positive, and moves forward. An empty compassion, on the other hand, includes flattery, that which is untrue and puffs up, only to be deflated at a later time. Encouragement is a firm word that has spine.

Systems Are Not People

True encouragement and compassion come from a fully invested person into another's life. It is important to note that systems, such as governmental or nonpersonal involvement are cold and distant. A 1–800 number is often an automatic recording to answer a high volume of calls. It is a system. When the recording or the voice on the tape says, "We care about you," it is hard to believe. You are still on hold, you still have to wait, and the person on the recording and the person that you need to talk too have no idea that you exist. It is a system for efficiency and not for relationship. Systems give way to efficiency and obligation to those who support them (tax payers or donors). The godly value is displaced to those who have power to keep an amoral system in place. Value and worth are redirected to the hierarchy rather than the people the system/church serves. The local church can erode Spirit-filled encouragement by allowing a system or program to devalue the people it reaches.

A system can be so efficient that it has an opposite effect. It can sow the seeds of anger in a person who desperately needs to talk to someone. It is as if they are experiencing rejection every time an electronic person "puts them off." Electronic communication is not "real" relationship building. We have fragile, emotionally immature people trying to connect "for real." It is no wonder that we have "really nice guys" going "postal" for apparently no reason at

18. Heb 12:5.
19. Rom 12:8; 1 Thess 4:18; Titus 2:6.

all. Compassion is sown consistently and steadily in real, flesh and blood, eye to eye, oral word exchange. The will of compassion is not felt with distance and easy electronic communication.

Our compassion can also be displaced by programs designed to make it easy for Christians to evangelize or disciple. American churches have long been dependent on gospel tracts to tell the good news of Jesus Christ without using living words. Sunday schools have been dependent on the curriculum provided for the whole study of the Sunday school lesson. No one should "throw the baby out with the bath water." Unless we are compassionate as God is, we will allow systems, methods, materials, and technology to cripple the outreach that God intended for us to do.

Empower the Church with Compassion, Mercy, and Encouragement

Christ's church dynamic is happening all around us. One time while having breakfast with my wife in a local restaurant I heard a lady across the dining room telling her husband about the latest truth she gained from a Bible study she went to. Next to us at another table, an older couple was giving a clear contextual presentation of the gospel to two young men who were Mormon missionaries. Another person paid for another's meal. These seemingly unconnected events are a part of the church dynamic. Multiple mini-stories of encouragement, mentorship, evangelism, kindness, and retelling of the greatness of God are going on all the time, "unofficially." Eternal actions rarely go into print or are publicly known. Compassion and encouragement are catalysts for greater things. Godly encouragement is a part of a father's love. There needs to be room for active compassionate encouragement in all our outreach to the world.

A sergeant pushes his soldiers forward confident of what they can do. Soldiers have no reason to doubt their leader in hardship because he has trained with them every step of the way. He has poured his life into them for a future day of testing on the battlefield. Encouragement is not done from afar. Encouraging words come from a voice of authority. A father's encouraging words are often based on experience. Experience through a life fully realized. Such is the need of the "fatherless." They are not in need of a cheerleading squad, for they already know that life can be hard and sorrowful. They are in need of someone with courage or strength, a truth teller, with words that are spoken with authority. Exhortation, drive, pushing, and motivation can only come from this kind of source. God expects us to practice true justice, kindness, and compassion to one another and to the unconnected fatherless, widows, and resident strangers.[20]

Mentorship: A "Go-To" Tool

An excellent methodology for encouragement is mentorship, whether formal or informal. It is a dynamic that many churches have been doing for centuries. Dr. Leonard Sax, who studies gender, observed our need generationally.

> One hundred years from now, scholars may look back at the disintegration of early twenty-first century culture and conclude that a fundamental cause for the unraveling of our social fabric was the neglect of gender in the raising of our children—not only in our schools, but also in the disbanding of gender—separate activities across generations, and in the near elimination of single-gender communal activities: women with girls, men with boys.[21]

In our fast-paced and compartmentalized society we neglect these basic dynamics of generational mentorship.

Donald Miller, who grew up without a dad, emphasizes the power of mentorship in the local church, saying, "I'm convinced hope for America lies with the church stepping in to mentor the fatherless."[22] Donald Miller, along with his local church, prayed and founded the Mentoring Project, a nonprofit organization that

20. Zech 7:9–10.
21. Sax, *Why Gender Matters*, 251.
22. Cockrel, "Solo Son," 59.

partners with local churches to mentor fatherless young men and promotes outreach ministry with mentorship.[23]

Leader-follower, disciple, or mentor all are ways of following a pattern to more maturity in Christ Jesus.[24] Pastor Adele Calhon describes mentorship this way:

> Mentoring does not need to be simply a professional and structured enterprise. Parents can mentor their children in skills and behaviors. Teachers can mentor their students. Students and friends can mentor one another when they have a skill someone wants. More mature married couples can mentor younger married couples, and older parents can mentor younger parents. Mentoring is passing on what you have. It does not require you to be responsible for more than you know.
>
> Few of us remember who won the last five Heisman trophies. We don't remember who wins the Nobel or Pulitzer prizes each year. But we all remember those mentors who believed in us and equipped us to become more than we ever could have been on our own.[25]

Purposeful and intentional encouragement is reflected in a program of mentorship.

An Early Mentor

I remember Mr. Lamb, now with the Lord, like it was yesterday. Yes, that is his real name (I think is made him tough like Johnny Cash's "Boy named Sue"). He had a Sunday school class full of rowdy sixth-grade boys. He had part of a finger missing, reflective of the hard-working men of the Northwest. The remarkable finger

23. The Mentoring Project, http://www.thementoringproject.org. (The Mentoring Project is an organization that exists to inspire and equip the faith community to provide positive male role models to boys between the ages of seven and fourteen. Founded in 2005, the Mentoring Project is the vision of Donald Miller, a bestselling author who resides in Portland, Oregon.)

24. Rom 12:2.

25. Calhoun, *Spiritual Disciplines Handbook*, 142–43.

was pointed at each of us lashing us with intense verbal love. As a preachers kid, I was privileged to be taught by him. He showed and used the discernment of the Holy Spirit in his life to me and the other boys. Although I had my rowdy moments, I was the "good" kid. If you are involved in a ministry of the church, a red flag should have gone off in your head. Whether you are an adult or a child we all seem to fall into the young prodigal or the older prodigal category (a lesson for another time). In our Bibles we know we all fall short of God's holy character. Patient Mr. Lamb would ask questions concerning the Bible lessons. Rowdy boys who were Christians would often give funny, "surface" answers and me being the token "know it all" preacher's kid, I would default to my standard three, I would say, "God," the "Holy Spirit," or the "church." The "Holy Spirit" answer in a Baptist church back then was intellectually classy stuff. But Mr. Lamb saw through all his boys. My memorable lesson came one day when he was internally grieved and frustrated by my standard "spiritual" answers. He verbally pinned me against the wall and made his point with the memorable finger God gave him for the teachable moments of a boy's life. "Dwight, I know you know more than you are sharing in class, I know you love Jesus Christ and from now on I will be expecting you to say more than pat answers." You would be right in concluding that this conversation is a paraphrase from my memory.

So it is with mentorship. What burns into the memory is God's love through that person, their personal conviction that you are valuable and special, a willingness to say hard things in loving ways, and a holder of a vision that you yourself have not yet seen. Soon after this encounter of love, I made a decision in seventh grade to go toward ministry, nothing specific, but it was specific enough in my walk with the Lord at that point in my life.

There are specific benefits of a "fatherhood" approach to mentoring. Francis Pleban and Keri Dietz describe the benefits that our generation is crying out for:

> The contributions of a father's mentoring efforts can include protection against risk behaviors, development of a

nurturing relationship, formation of prosocial behavior, and development of mastery.[26]

Mentorship labeled appropriately for the cultural community it reaches out to can be an effective tool in reaching those who have lost someone of strength to give direction and spiritual orientation. Mentorship is another way of saying discipleship or encouragement. It is at the heart of the church's "great commission." Dr. Joshua Kang emphasizes the duality of our mission. "Making a disciple out of a convert is necessary, but it's costly in time and effort."[27] A convert is the start of an incredible investment from the saints of God. Our fatherless outreach filter includes compassion, mercy, and encouragement.

26. "Fathers as Mentors: Bridging the Gap between Generations," in Brotherson and White, *Why Fathers Count*, 313.

27. Kang, *Scripture by Heart*, 75.

Leadership Study Questions

1. Have we a compassionate representation of God in our community?

   Define compassion. What is it about compassion we usually miss? (See Zech 7:9–10.)

   "For he says to Moses, "I will have _____ on whom I have _____, and I will have _____ on whom I have _____." It does not, therefore, depend on man's desire or effort, but on God's _____" (Rom 9:15–16).

2. Does our church exercise compassion with heart, mind, and will?

3. Do we have programs and methods that represent and express godly compassion?

4. Does our corporate compassion draw (invite) the broken, hurt, and disenfranchised from our community? (See 2 Cor 5:14a.)

5. Is compassion reflected in our missions, worship, and local church outreach?

6. Is there a compassionate vision in our ministry goals?

7. Do we have systems (1–800 numbers, money without interaction, programs that are popular but without the good news of Jesus Christ, programs that no one remembers why they were started and who they are ministering to) rather than people meeting needs?

8. Is compassion taught or caught in our local church?

For Next Week

Read the next chapter.

- Read the "fatherless" passages.

- Pray for compassion to be seen in your local church ministry.
- Identify your church's teaching (word and deed) of compassion.

6

Authority

For the LORD your God is God of gods and Lord of lords, the great
God, mighty and awesome, who shows no partiality and accepts no
bribes. He defends the cause of the fatherless and widow, and loves
the alien, giving him food and clothing. And you are to love those who
are aliens, for you yourselves were aliens in Egypt. Fear the LORD your
God and serve him. Hold fast to him and take your oaths in his name.

—DEUTERONOMY 10:17–20

All the people were amazed and said to each other, "What is this
teaching? With authority and power he gives orders to evil spirits and
they come out!"

—LUKE 4:36

The "A" Word, What Is It?

Authority is another word for stewarded power. God has commanded, determined, chosen, and instructed us with his authority

to pay attention and do actions that reflect his person. Dads likewise command, determine, decide, and instruct daughters and sons based on the authority given them by God. A dad is to measure up to the desires of God in influencing individuals, families, and communities. A lawful society commands lawfulness, order, and common decency based on the authority that God, and its own structural norms, has bestowed upon its leaders.

Our forty-three "fatherless" passages are founded in the law of God, the Torah.[1]

By the nature of the word "fatherless," God expects his institution of the family to be grounded in his guidelines. Our authority, or power, to father in the darkness of "fatherlessness" is given only by our Creator and Lawmaker, God our Father.

Authority can be an unpopular word. Most see it as unwanted constraint to their life. From my chaplaincy experience, this often separates out a career soldier from the general population of America. Soldiers willingly work under authority. *Webster's College Dictionary* defines authority as "the power to determine, adjudicate, or otherwise settle issues: the right to control, command, or determine." *Strong's Concordance* defines authority in reference to Jesus Christ: "a privilege, force, capacity, competency, freedom, or mastery; delegated *influence*: —authority, jurisdiction, liberty, power, right, and strength." The definition differs from Webster because it has the thread of stewardship of strength given. The church does not conjure up its own strength. *Strong's Concordance* defines in Greek the word authority, stating that *exousia* (authority) is a power to act. Its definition is expressed as power, authority, and weight, and especially: moral authority, influence.[2] A leader who fails to recognize authority as a stewardship can become a very dangerous and self-serving individual. In a role as a military chaplain our prayer at military change of commands is given to recognize that God is the ultimate grantor of all power and au-

---

1. Deut 10:17–20. God expects us to steward strength and compassion toward the fatherless, widows, and the alien as he does. Isa 10:1–4 shows that God expects power to be stewarded toward the poor, widows, and fatherless.

2. See Luke 4:36.

thority. With every transition of command or leadership, we should seek leaders that see the power granted as a responsibility of stewardship. The same is applicable to spiritual leaders. Many commanders, to a greater or lesser degree, recognize that authority and power are granted from God, the American Constitution, higher rank, and positional responsibility. A governmental leader who swears on the Bible is admitting that there is a God of power above them. Just because these ceremonial tokens of tradition are in place is not a guarantee of a leader looking at power as a stewardship. But this is our prayer as followers.

Authority Comes from Where?

The contexts of all our "fatherless" Scripture passages show a lack of significant authoritative relationships in people's lives. Each people group God points out lacks a powerful support from another person or group: the alien lacks the support of a culture and set of norms; the widow lacks the support of a husband; the children lack the support of a father. The stewardship of authority is a foregone conclusion in order to bring power to the powerless. Actions that God expects the church to take on behalf of the outcast people groups are justice, vindication, compassion, mercy, and encouragement. Whether the action of a hard or soft word, we minister best with authority from God, given to Jesus Christ, and delegated to us through multiple methods of local church outreach. Dr. Angus Paddison explains,

> The authority which Christians prioritize has its origins within the triune fellowship and is mediated to the world through the Son to whom 'all authority has been given' (Mt. 28:18) and through the Spirit who allows us a share in the mission of the Son. This distribution of authority is through a host of mundane objects and institutions, each elected to participate in the authority of God—the practices of the church, tradition, Scripture, worship and preaching, although of course the precise individual status of these different sources of authority and the

calibration among them varies across different Christian traditions.[3]

Paddison goes on, in his text, to warn churches of the danger of practicing authority without acknowledging God as the source of all power.

Churches are working hard at a possession of equality[4] and inclusiveness[5] in ecclesiastical doctrine and polity; both are absent from creation's power to grasp and maintain. Only in the context of a loving Creator can these elements possibly exist and be defined. In churches and academia alike seeking to fall in line with the politics of government, these concepts are boldly propagated as an official spiritual teaching, effectively bringing an imbalance to doctrine and ultimately their local church outreach. Often studies of "authority" have a social presupposition in mind when they try to define God's authority for us. Always go back to the Word of God for your definition of authority. There are many who have their own experimental agenda for the church.

The world understands power structures. The weak need a handle, someone or a community to look up to who has strength. We all work together better when there is a community understanding of power. Education, sociology, psychology, business, and the military (to name a few) all study and recognize "powers that be." Theology is weak when one has no clarity concerning the personhood and power of God. Theology is inconsistent when one defines terms based on feeling, passionate causes, personality bents, and human will.

Attractive Authority

As of this writing, I work with juvenile boys, whose ages vary from fourteen to seventeen. They come from a variety of backgrounds with an assortment of charges that brought them to the residential

3. Paddison, "Authority of Scripture," 448–49.

4. Phil 2:6–7.

5. Exod 19:5–6a; Deut 14:2; Titus 2:14; 1 Pet 2:9.

care facility for treatment. Many come to us angry and often at a loss on how to control their emotions, hormones, words, etc. Together as a staff we model appropriate words, actions, and talk through methodology that will help them navigate through life. Through consistency and repetitive reinforcement of what "right" looks like, we have an opportunity to correct some of the abuses of power from their past and show appropriate choices to prevent a cycle of the same abuse in the future. The people of God are to be this kind of witness in the stewardship of power.

Authority needs to be presented as an attractive stewardship of power. The fatherless lens of "authority" is God saying to us to be strong,[6] be a defender of the weak,[7] stand for justice,[8] be angry and sin not,[9] be an encouragement (meaning pour your courage into another). Defenseless and helpless people need a person of power to lean on for healing and to be a model of strength to give them back some power to call their own, dignity, and a correct self-worth.[10]

For too long, helpless people have been abused by those who have set themselves up to be an authority in their lives—including the church.

When serving in the military in Columbia, South America, we saw young men in Bogota approached by two powers. Either the drug cartel or the government will ask for a commitment to their kind of power; a power to serve a drug cartel or a government that uses power to stop it. In a country where there is a lack of opportunity for youth, whoever gets to them first will decide which way they go for the rest of their lives. Whether in another country or ours, this is the precipice that the powerless or the victims of unchecked power are sitting on.

Ultimately, those that seek or desire strength will flee to where they perceive it will help them. If God's people are to reach the

6. Deut 10:18–19.
7. Ps 82:3.
8. Deut 24:17–21.
9. Eph 4:26.
10. Rom 8:37.

hurting, voiceless, and powerless people of the world, we need to be responsible with God-delegated power. Churches are to be holy examples of the power of God transforming people's lives. Good authority is grounded in who God is. A Father to the fatherless: a steady guide, a source of strength, a clear direction, a faithful God. The saints of the church exude this in their lives and the broken will be drawn to this power.

Correct Use of Authority

Authority is such a potent word. One who has many experiences in the local church will tie his or her most negative event to that particular word, "authority." A positive or a negative experience can forever define spiritual authority for that person. A misuse of authority, especially among those who represent God in leadership, will have devastating effects. Says Paul Vitz, author of *Faith of the Fatherless: The Psychology of Atheism,*

> Many people are aware of how particular experiences with representatives of God, Christianity, or the Church affect their religious belief. For example, I knew of a man who had been an atheist for much of his life, but eventually came back to Christianity as a member of the Episcopal church. He had left the Catholic Church and rejected God because of a particular painful experience: when he made his First Communion, he accidently dropped the Host and was publicly chastised, indeed humiliated, by the priest. He felt the wound so deeply that he lost his faith. There are, no doubt, many examples of the behavior of those who supposedly represent God causing such wounds. It is important, however, to keep in mind that however natural and human such reactions are, they are not rational, but psychological.[11]

While churches minimize poor authoritative leadership by use of administrative tools (screen, verify, vet, question, and perform background checks), a lot of the interpersonal wrongs in

11. Vitz, *Faith of the Fatherless*, 157–58.

the stewardship of authority can be further minimized with God's mandates to repent, forgive, and restore relationships. Prayerful dependence on God, a practice of spiritual discernment, and a Spirit-filled corporate consensus on leadership decisions is the practice of proper authority. These practices will bring the church closer to the heart of God.

Authority is a combination of power, responsibility, accountability, leadership, and intentional ministry. Many Christian writings avoid the word "authority." Often Christian writings, in order to gain a hearing, stay away from this word that brings with it strong reactions. I would also postulate that the word smacks against our cherished self. The bent in all of us is to be at the center. It is the inclination of a willful humanity.[12]

Authority is crucial in tough times, both individually and corporately. In the crucibles of trials and hardship, hurting people look to a power that can help in the most desperate of times. As the created we often look to a proof that legitimizes that power.

The struggle that the American communities of faith have in their ecclesiastical polity with power and authority is that it looks and feels unspiritual and ungodly. The larger persecuted church has no time for such debates and has simply delegated authority given to those seen as called of God.[13] There is a grittiness that accompanies those who wade into the hurt of the world. Stories that do not fit with our "happy ending" view of the Christian life. The Christian nurse uses her power to hold a baby or the hand of an elderly person who are alone and near death, to be Jesus Christ in those moments. The Baptist chaplain chooses to baptize the dead baby of a grieving mother because his own correct doctrine is not what Jesus Christ would address in that moment. A chaplain or pastor hugging an angry teenager firmly because he just found out his dad died for his country is the Jesus power for the moment. The Christian corrections officer who endures the cursing of an inmate "drying out" or "coming off" a substance to be Jesus Christ in the moment of helplessness. Yet, there are Christians

---

12. Rom 3:23.
13. See Yun, *Heavenly Man.*

who believe that the power of God is a high-tech, well-organized, well-synchronized, high-powered motivational speaker event where you can "feel the spirit of God moving." Unfortunately, I have heard such comments after speaking as a one-time event speaker. Heaven help us! Our worship service is not the only place to experience the power of God. Our altar calls are not God's measurement of the church's effectiveness.

The word "authority" calls us to look holistically at the stewardship of power. Jesus Christ was given power by God[14] He delegated it to the disciples who also understood it was given.[15] Our prime example in the exercise of authority is Jesus Christ; he is the head of the church. The more we mirror him the better we can carry our stewardship of authority. Nathan Shaw brings us back to Jesus' example:

> Some people carry authority in such a way as to make others feel very small. Is this true of you and me? If so, we are not following the example of our Lord. From what we read about Jesus, the opposite was true. Jesus did not look down on people. He confronted supercilious religious attitudes and those who were propagating them but treated people with the utmost solicitude and sensitivity.[16]

Our stewardship of authority is given by Jesus Christ through the living, breathing organism of the church body.[17] As we see Jesus lived out in the membership of our churches we then choose our spiritual leadership according to how they handle the stewardship and responsibility of power.

Authority is given to local church leadership by recognizing the multiple qualities God emphasizes from Scripture, fervent in prayer and faithful to serving God by serving others.[18] Faithful-

---

14. Mark 9:7; 11:27–33; John 1:1–4.

15. Luke 24:49; Acts 8:20.

16. Shaw, *Least of These*, 33.

17. Rom 12:3–8.

18. Gal 5:22–26. Aside from gifts, the fruit of the Spirit is an excellent showing of authority in walking with God. Verse 26 reminds us not to have

ness is a reflective observation. Authority takes time and proof.[19] Pride and resentment of others being over you is the very nature of Satan; we cannot persevere in godly fellowship with this kind of poison. That is why we take most of our prayer concerns to our long-time faithful elders. Their experience gives us grounding and perspective. They have been walking with God a long time.[20] All authority is given and recognized.[21]

Yes, Authority Can Have "Push Back"

By what right do we insert our authority into a disenfranchised person's life? As saints of God we often cower at the first sight of pushback. This, however, is a good sign that one is in the right place. Hurt people push back because they have been disappointed, abused, taken advantage of and are disoriented because life has disappointed them. Nathan Shaw again points to the early church as a model to understand the experience of powerlessness:

> I believe it is significant that, when it came to appointing disciples to sort out the dispute concerning the widows, men were chosen for the job and not women. Having no husbands to look out for them, the widows were in need of the protection and authority of godly men. This is a key point for our understanding of the plight of widows and the fatherless today—particularly when these individuals have known only abusive authority from men, something that happens all too often. Those who are vulnerable need to be protected—not controlled or dictated to, but protected.[22]

Our negative use or memory of authority can be replaced with God's teaching and positive examples of authority. His call to

strife in roles God puts us in. "Let us not be conceited, provoking and envying each other."

19. 1 Tim 3:6.

20. Jas 5:16.

21. Matt 28:18; John 17:2; Rom 13:1.

22. Shaw, *Least of These*, 68.

minister to the brokenness of this world demands the strength of godly authority.

Remember where a Christian's authority comes from. First our authority comes from God and his work in saving us, just as Israel was saved from Egypt.[23] Second, authority comes from Jesus Christ the head of his church.[24] Third, authority comes from his commands in the Word of God.[25] It is by God's authority that we live a godly life.[26]

In the early days of this writer's ministry, my dad would coach me in the reading of Scripture in the large auditorium of Medford First Baptist Church. (It was our annual practice for the youth group to take and lead an evening service.) The big lesson remembered when trying to instill oratory confidence in his son: "Dwight, when you read the Word of God, you are walking on the most firm foundation you can walk on!" This echo's in my memory. Methods, stories, humor, and great outlines cannot go wandering off far from the text of Scripture or we are on shaky and unstable ground. The Word of God is powerful and is a two-edged sword that does surgery on our heart and offensively provides an answer to the devil's schemes.

Leadership and outreach ministries that reflect the heart-beat and authority of God choose to support his priorities. Many churches support people and organizations that have nothing to do with the "great commission" that Jesus Christ delegated to us.[27] One would be hard pressed to find the good news of Jesus Christ being the largest priority in America's top fifty charities.[28] Giving alone cannot bring restoration. The local church is God's catalyst to restore the relationship between God and humanity. God will hold us accountable for the authority that has been granted us.

23. Exod 22:21; Rom 1:16–17.

24. Eph 2:19–22.

25. John 14:23–24.

26. 1 Thess 4:7–8.

27. Matt 28:18–20; Mark 16:15; Luke 24:49; and Acts 1:7–8. Note: All "Great Commission" passages.

28. See "America's Top 50 Charities," *Christian Science Monitor*, 2013.

Godly authority is a factor in our fatherless lens. We should not be willful contributors to efforts that merely prop up humanity rather than exalt God almighty.

Why is authority an important "fatherless" factor in local church ministry outreach? It is so much like a father to guide sons and daughters in the area of strength, responsibility, stewardship, and a firm encouraging loving direction. A father pours out his own courage and strength, and models responsibility for his precious children. Likewise, the power we wield and represent in the church cannot be faulty when we reach our hand out to the helpless and the disenfranchised. Proper authority brings continuity, consistency, and calm. If our ministry in any way takes advantage of the people we minister to, God will be removing the light from our lampstand.[29]

29. Rev 2:5.

Leadership Study Questions

1. Have we an excellent representation of God's authority in our local church? Define authority.

   "All the people were amazed and said to each other, 'What is this teaching? With _____ and _____ he gives orders to evil spirits and they come out!'" (Luke 4:36).

2. Does our church have well-defined and documented authority? (E.g., leaders who have walked with God a long time; recognition of Jesus Christ as head of the church; the Word of God as that which guides all important decisions.)

3. Do we have programs and methods that represent and express godly authority?

4. Does our church know and express God's power in clear teaching?

5. Is God's authority reflected in our missions, worship, and local church outreach?

6. Is there an authoritative vision in our ministry goals? (Who and what do we base our outreach?)

7. Why do the fatherless, widow, alien, disenfranchised, down trodden, etc., need authority? Are they attracted to our stewardship of power?

8. How is the personal power given to you by God holding another person up in a time of great powerlessness?

9. Is a proper authority taught in our local church?

For Next Week

Read the next chapter.

- Read the "fatherless" passages.

- Pray for authority to be seen as God defines it in your local church ministry.

- Identify your church's teaching (word and deed) on authority.

7

Relationship

When you have finished setting aside a tenth of all your produce in the
third year, the year of the tithe, you shall give it to the Levite, the alien,
the fatherless and the widow, so that they may eat in your towns and
be satisfied.

—DEUTERONOMY 26:12–13

When Jesus reached the spot, he looked up and said to him, "Zacchaeus, come down immediately. I must stay at your house today."

—LUKE 19:5

In our forty-three Scripture passages we see people unconnected
and short-changed in the area of relationships. God's eyesight
sees people, not things, as most important. Relationships on earth
communicate who God is. Deuteronomy emphasizes not only
the provision of food, but the inclusion of those without connection to be included within the community during celebrations
and special holy days. The word "satisfaction" in Deuteronomy
26:12–13 means to be full; suffice; have enough; in the context of

community. Filling a belly is not enough. There is a connection to God first, then people and communities. Say Neal Krause and David Hayward,

> The finding from our study further indicated that awe of God is associated with greater life satisfaction. Moreover, the relationship between the two is wholly due to feelings of connectedness with others. . . . So taken together, our study provided support for a conceptual sequence that begins with church attendance and wisdom, operates through feelings of connectedness with others, and concludes with relating connectedness with others and life satisfaction.[1]

Satisfaction for the poor is not just feeding the belly but connecting the soul to a godly community; it is a connection that emulates a loving Father God.

When God looks at the fatherless, he sees the need of a fatherhood relationship. Ministry outreach is to involve committed and firm relationships. Drs. Henry and Richard Blackaby emphasize relationship as a priority in spiritual leadership:

> The ultimate goal of spiritual leadership is not to achieve numerical results, to accomplish tasks with perfection, or to grow for growth's sake. It is to take their people from where they are to where God wants them to be. God's primary concern for people is not results but relationship. Calling comes before vocation. There is a profound comment on this issue in Exodus 19:4: "You have seen what I did to the Egyptians and how I carried you on eagles' wings and brought you to Me.[2]

When God looks to the broken, he sees the need of restored relationship. Not just a steady relationship but also helping others who are unconnected to restore their broken relationships. It is on the basis of a restored relationship with a Holy God that we have the power to help others.

---

1. Krause and Hayward, "Assessing," 1–9.
2. Blackaby and Blackaby, *Spiritual Leadership*, 127-28.

Quality Elements of Relationship

A father relationship involves remembering where one came from, commitment, and faithful follow-through. The godly examples of mentorship, prayer warriors, fathers and mothers of children, teachers, etc., all have these things in common. Influence will occur with modeling, commitment, and time invested. Daniel Bayse in his handbook for helping volunteers build relationships with prisoners tells of five concepts that he claims, if taught, will end criminal careers. If we are on the freedom side of the bars, perhaps we take some of these for granted:

1. *Teach them how to love.*

2. *Teach them how to forgive.*

3. *Give them the gift of self-esteem.*

4. *Teach them the keys to freedom.*

    (a) respecting the rules of society and

    (b) taking responsibility for one's own actions.

5. *Teach them to dream.*[3]

We need to ask ourselves, do we have an environment for relationships that allows for time, modeling, and long time commitment? Crowds, numbers, and excitement are not guarantees that their loneliness has been eradicated. It is possible to be gimmicky within relationship building. Just look at Facebook as an example. Here is a ready-made inflated view of friendship that does not touch the depth of a relationship and authentic friendship. The taste of the bonds of Christian kinship will be a stark contrast to the world's controlling, manipulating, and shallow friendships. A rightly functioning father relationship-oriented church will draw the orphan, widow, and the disenfranchised. Orphaned at age twelve, John Fawcett captures the church's body life in pen and song during his faithful pastorate of fifty-four years in the same church:

3. Bayse, *Helping Hands*, 55–56.

Blest be the tie that binds our hearts in Christian love:
The fellowship of kindred minds is like to that above.

Before our Father's throne we pour our ardent prayers;
our fears, our hopes, our aims are one, our comforts and
our cares.

We share each other's woes, our mutual burdens bear,
and often for each other flows the sympathizing tear.

When we asunder part, it gives us inward pain; but we
shall still be joined in heart, and hope to meet again.

At one time John Fawcett tried to leave the church that he was
stewarding as pastor, but found it too painful to leave it for the very
reasons he had written about in this familiar song.[4]

Let's Start Healing Relationships

Pastors suffering burnout and leaving churches after only a handful of years may be due to the fact that too many churches represent brokenness rather than mended relationships. The painful experience of a broken relationship inside a church is remembered more than the bittersweet pain of a congregation who send one of their own saints out to the mission field. Christ followers are tempted to move from one church to another rather than sticking with a relationship and learning the mending and healing properties that Jesus Christ taught us in Scripture: affirmation, blessing, confession, faithfulness, focusing on the things above, forgiveness, redemption, remembering our first love, and thankfulness.

The Church Is to Reflect God's Healed Relationships

Especially with such emptiness of fatherhood in our nation, our churches need to reflect strength in the relationships that come its way with God's power. We can be surrogate fathers in the wake of

4. Peterson and Peterson, *Complete Book of Hymns*, 266–67.

the destruction of the family. Dr. Kent Hughes points to what we need to step into such a role:

> Our society is awash with millions of daughters pathetically seeking the affection their fathers never gave them—and some of these daughters are at the sunset of their lives. In the extreme, there are myriads of sons who were denied a healthy same-sex relationship with their father and are now spending the rest of their lives in search of their sexual identity via perversion and immorality.[5]

We are to be intentional in our relationships to provide a picture of godly fatherhood. For men, it's not just making a baby that makes you a father. It is the constant, daily responsibility of loving, caring, disciplining, providing, correcting, and encouraging that creates stable individuals. Some church programs seem to be designed to keep fatherhood relationships at a distance. A program can add numbers, be entertaining, and cause a big commotion, but all the while lack long-term faithful relationship building. The church is to be different in programs and systems by always including the dynamic of relationship building. Steve Corbett and Brian Fikkert are both associate professors at Covenant College. Brian, founder and executive director of Chalmers Center for Economic Development, states:

> Poor people are often at the mercy of systems created by the powerful. Hence, poverty-alleviation efforts need to address both broken systems and broken individuals, using highly relational approaches wherever possible.[6]

Local churches need to regularly evaluate their systems and programs to make sure that they are not sterile and void of relationship dynamics.

Why does God's heart see the fatherless of the nations? He has made everyone in his image. God is the master of relationship dynamics in friendship, church body life, and family. God's template

---

5. Hughes, *Disciplines*, 47.
6. Corbett and Fikkert, *When Helping Hurts*, 185.

of family relationships are prosperous and prevent destruction if properly understood and maintained according to his decrees.

Our sin is responsible for the pain, turmoil, and destruction that come to many family structures.[7] God sent his Son, Jesus Christ, to die to bring salvation to all mankind. The healing of relationships on earth is to be reflective of that supreme restoration. This means that our heart cries and reaches out just as his does.[8] A people who know God and his salvation in their lives will reach out to those who have suffered loss. Those who enjoy close intimate relationship with God or family cannot enjoy it knowing that a person within their area of influence is without a godly relationship that makes them whole. In fact, the lack of a relationship or a person who is void of intimate human relationships is to be as painful to us as it is to God. It tugs at his heart and therefore those who belong to him will feel their heart breaking as well. The lack of a healthy relationship as God intended is the foundational start of multiple problems that will occur in a fatherless life. Pamela Thomas, from experience and study, comments on the fears of a fatherless woman:

> In no other area of a fatherless daughter's life do the emotional legacies of father loss come into play more dramatically than in her romantic relationships with men. The fear of abandonment triggers the fear of intimacy and sex; an inability to trust men; problems with self-esteem; difficulties with assertiveness and establishing appropriate boundaries; conflicting feelings relating to dependency, separation, and commitment; and sometimes inappropriate shame.[9]

In our world today there is a lack of real building and investing in relationships. A group of people is not necessarily the most necessary dynamic of relationship building. Lonely people exist in crowds of thousands. Investment and the sharing of oneself are crucial in relationship building—a transparency that assures

7. McGeady, *God Has a Kid's Face.*
8. Job 31:16–23; Ps 10:14.
9. Thomas, *Fatherless Daughters,* 159.

a person of a fair exchange of worth and validation. The church holds the power of restoration because it knows God intimately. Mercy Amba Oduyoye is a Methodist theologian known for her work with African women in religion and culture at Trinity Theological Seminary in Ghana. Her passion is to speak for voiceless African women; she speaks to the church's role for all the voiceless:

> People who come to Church love and respect the Church. What they hear in Church should make them go out and be the Church, not just make them feel good about themselves. The poor and the voiceless who still come to Church, come seeking community, and the power to continue to live, and the opportunity for participation in the only place where they have been made to believe their humanity is honored.[10]

The living, breathing organism of the church is dynamic under the control of the Lord Jesus Christ. The church is to embrace the power of restored relationship.

While the church looks at easy programmable ideas to get people in the door, Jesus beckons us to open the door and enter into relationships based on the eternal one we have with him. John Sowers, president of the Mentoring Project writes:

> Many counselors agree that healthy and loving human relationships are the most powerful behavior modifier in the world. Fatherless children lack these loving relationships and often feel lonely, flawed, and incomplete. It is in relationships where the fatherless generation has been wounded the most deeply. Thus, it is in relationships where reconciliation must begin.[11]

Families and churches are to be a well of strong relationships to which broken people come and quench their thirst. Programs that invite the growth of healthy "relationship" building are often long term commitments. Individuals that come and visit with

---

10. Oduyoye, *Stones Will Cry Out*, 122.

11. Sowers, *Fatherless Generation*, 97.

great need will see a path to the development of relationships. Our fatherless outreach lens includes healthy "relationship" building.

Leadership Study Questions

1. Do we develop godly relationships in our local church?

2. What is satisfaction? Does food and money given to a need produce satisfaction?

3. Does our church have a well-defined plan to develop relationships (with the poor, the down and out, unsaved, the saved, in discipleship)?

4. Do we have programs and methods that represent and express godly relationships?

5. Does our church teach and express what godly relationships look like?

6. Is God's priority of relationships reflected in our missions, worship, and local church outreach?

7. Why do the fatherless, widow, alien, disenfranchised, down trodden, etc., need relationship? Are they attracted to relationships within our church?

8. What are the elements needed to develop godly relationships (time, commitment, initiation, determination, etc.)?

9. If Jesus chose Zacchaeus to have a relationship with, what does that say to us in how we are to choose relationships? "When Jesus reached the spot, he looked up and said to him, "Zacchaeus, come down immediately. I _____ stay at your house today" (Luke 19:5–6).

For Next Week

Read the next chapter.

- Read the "fatherless" passages.
- Pray for relationships to be seen as God defines it in your local church ministry.
- Identify your church's teaching (word and deed) on godly relationships.

8

Presence

Religion that God our Father accepts as pure and faultless is this: to look after orphans and widows in their distress and to keep oneself form being polluted by the world.

—JAMES 1:27

Therefore go and make disciples of all nations, baptizing them in the name of the Father and of the Son and of the Holy Spirit, and teaching them to obey everything I have commanded you. And surely I am with you always to the very end of the age.

—MATTHEW 28:19–20

The "less" in fatherless is our exhortation to draw near to the hurting. The fatherless lack the presence of a father. The widow lacks the presence of a husband. The stranger lacks the presence of a friend. All people groups do well to have the presence of loving relationships as a source of strength and encouragement. A loving presence sets relationships up for success. Studies have found that regardless of a father's educational achievement, his presence alone brings strength, discipline, guidance, and encouragement to his children.[1] God's commands from Scripture beckon us to reach the fatherless with presence. *Presence matters. Presence is a choice.* Dr. Erickson observes this in the ungodly action of fatherlessness:

> All father hunger springs from one main source: desertion. A father's abdication may be total or emotional or what the individual experiences as desertion. There are seven specific causes of father loss: death, divorce, single mothering, adoption, addiction, abuse and traditional fathering. The common element with all but one is the *father's choice* to absent himself.[2]

Observe that intentional presence and not just physical presence is a great need of the downtrodden. Dr. Ken Canfield rounds out our ministry exhortation of intentional presence by pointing out another glaring aspect of fatherlessness:

> When most adults think of fatherlessness, they see children raised without fathers due to divorce, abandonment, and premature death of the father. Indeed, more that 19 million children in America—nearly 40 percent—are growing up without their biological fathers. That is a tragic and devastating figure. But I wonder: How high would that figure be if it included children whose fathers are physically present, but emotionally distant or absent?[3]

One can only imagine. Therefore, presence in ministry is to be intentional and not accidental. It is no accident that God points to those in society that represent the most need, demand the most effort, and take a seemingly incredible amount of time.

Gordon MacDonald causes us to take stock of the people groups we surround ourselves with and ask questions of introspection:

1. See Mackey and Mackey, "Father Presence."
2. Erickson, *Longing for Dad*, 55.
3. Canfield, *Heart of a Father*, 129–30.

I find it easy to be present—doesn't everyone?—to attractive people, advantaged people, visionary people, intelligent people, likeable people. I love being present to people who like me and find me witty and charming. My grandchildren fit this category.

But present to people who are weak, poor, sick, grumpy, unreliable, unthankful, and disrespectful? That's another story. My instinct is, all too often, to be absent to them. . . . Sometimes I win; often I lose in this being present business. Because being present to people means that I must listen extra carefully, listen, and then respond. And that can be inconvenient and too taxing.[4]

The Slight Difference

The spiritual practice and ministry of presence is slightly different than just relationship building. "A friend loves at all times, and a brother is born for adversity."[5] Dr. Robert Alden, my Old Testament seminary professor, lover of God's Word, now with the Lord, wrote:

> Most scholars agree verse 17 is a synonymous parallel instead of a contrast between friend and brother; both are there when you need them. Friends are sometimes even closer than relatives (cf. 18:24; 27:10), but hopefully relatives are also friends. Both, in any case, are needed for support and encouragement, especially during hard times.[6]

Presence is more powerful with a track record of faithfulness in relationship, proofs of commitment, and family connection.

Some brokenness in our communities simply has no answers. It is beyond words, and overwhelms our comprehension. Chaplains/pastors are often called to this ministry of crises where

4. MacDonald, *Building Below the Waterline*, 12–13.
5. Prov 17:17.
6. Alden, *Proverbs*, 135–36.

a "Christ follower" is thrust into the chaos and by the destructive forces of sin. Only the relationship connection that was invested in before the horrible "event" allows the person representing Christ into the crucible of suffering. Pastor Adele Ahlberg Calhoun comments on Christ's example in such cases:

> Jesus was never a lone ranger. He has always been a part of a divine community with the Father and the Holy Spirit. And when he came to earth, he continued to live his life in small groups. He began his ministry by choosing twelve disciples to be with him (Luke 6:13). Then he spent three years pouring himself into this small group. He taught them truth about God and about themselves. He modeled spiritual practices for and with them. He introduced them to the experiences of service, witness and healing prayer. And day after relentless day, in the messy, hard-to-control center of community, he gave them the gift of his full presence.[7]

The presence of Jesus Christ is that call in the middle of the night or that meeting with someone difficult on one's day off. It is death, sickness, and shocking hardship showing up unannounced. It is being there for the mentally challenged person who asks the same questions, gives the same greetings, and reminds us of the one aspect of God they know about over and over again. God wants us to go out of our way to see the "fatherless," the hurt, the pain, the uncontrollable and overwhelming sense of loss in its many forms.

The outreach of ministry inserts God into unanswerable and unfixable ordeals of life. As military chaplains we often faced the challenge of "presence" in the hard mission of death notification, an official tasking that has specific military protocols and procedures. The command does the hardest part in the sense that the person who is the command representative speaks the bad news. The chaplain is the compassionate arm of the command. The contrast is an example of the tension experienced in ministry. Be there, speak truth (sugar coating prolongs pain), commit to walking with

---

7. Calhoun, *Spiritual Disciplines Handbook*, 149.

them in the shadow of death.[8] Those who are "called" to ministry are thrust into seemingly impossible God-dependent situations.[9] Yet the downtrodden and broken hearted are depending upon a "God walker" in moments of overwhelming grief and turmoil.

Nope, No Super Hero Costume

A person can be a minister of the presence of God and not feel very powerful. Likewise they can also see God move and use them in unimaginable ways they never envisioned. The experience of ministering in death or pain in a hospital can illustrate these truths. There is a temptation to fill the void of overwhelming pain and grief with words. In the midst of death notifications and hospital visits; in the middle of doubting about the right words of comfort; in the medium of "empty-not-very-well-thought-out" words; the "words" are rarely remembered. The next temptation in overwhelming pain is to project or reach for one's own similar experience to bring comfort and it ends up doing just the opposite, minimizing the hurt person's experience and only validating the caregiver's need to know he or she is being compassionate. Presence is often all that is needed and "I dare say, demanded." Presence is powerful.[10]

The ministry of presence is a handle to the overwhelmed and brokenhearted.

An Example of Presence

While ministering to boys in the inner city of Portland, Oregon and going to Multnomah University, I stayed with my friend

8. Facts are based upon my experience of approximately forty-five to fifty death notifications in the military; contrary to popular belief, one does not remember them all. Some over others tear your heart out depending on your triggers (mine is children and newly married spouses). Some take longer to process and their grief is a part of your spiritual journey.

9. Lieberman et al., *Losing a Parent*, 26–29.

10. Ps 31:20; 139:7; Jude 24.

Dennis for part of that time. Dennis would sit on the front porch of his home with a boy whose father was an alcoholic and whose mother was a prostitute. This little boy often came home to a dark and lonely home. His bed was an old used mattress thrown on the floor. His parents kept him for their benefit because they knew the overburdened system and pulled together a good show for the welfare workers. Dennis's ministry was to sit on his front porch and listen until the late hours, lend strength and courage, and weep with the little boy. Dennis had his own family of two boys and a girl, a loving wife, ministry goals, work, and going to school to focus on. He had plenty of valid reasons not to reach out, but on the other hand, he knew he was so blessed by God that it made sense to share the presence of God with the "fatherless." Jesus Christ's salvation continues to work his purposes in lives we have touched. As long as we have breath, each story, each touch, each word, and each step of obedience moves God's salvation story forward. God takes our lives touched by the grace of God and infuses them into his world for his glory. As the saints of old, you may never see your Spirit-filled efforts realized in this life.

Are We Present Where God Wants Us?

Dr. Mark Strong, a pastor in Portland, Oregon, connects the importance of presence to fatherhood:

> In the New Testament, God is portrayed as a good father who provides for the needs of his children. He is a father who blesses his children in a context of a loving and intimate relationship. His character reflects his faithfulness, continuing presence, mercy, love, knowledge of his children's lives and ability to provide.[11]

The ministry of presence is a shepherd's way of walking in the spiritual life.[12] We follow the promptings of the Holy Spirit when individuals are laid heavy upon one's heart. The local church

11. Strong, *Church for the Fatherless*, 94.
12. See Carnes, "Like Sheep without a Shepherd."

feels sensitivity to its membership and outreach. Dr. Mark Dever, president of 9 Marks Ministry, states,

> So if a congregation has not set its eyes upon an individual for months, even years, how can it testify that that person is faithfully running the race? If an individual is missing in action but has not joined some other Bible-believing church, how do we know if he or she was really a part of us (see John 2:19)? We don't necessarily know that such uninvolved people are not Christians: we simply can't affirm that they are.[13]

Do we have shepherding questions? Have we visited our infirmed? Have we found out why certain members have been missing for a while? Are our prayers well informed as to the struggles our saints are going through? Are our ministry and prayers intentional in the practice of bringing the presence of God to the hurting, lonely, and disheartened? The answers measure intentional presence.

Listening, a "Go-To" Tool for Being Present

Presence and sensitivity to the broken and oppressed start with a very simple method: listening to people one on one. Within the practice of legitimate listening, many nuances of strength are communicated. A space is given to acceptance. A person's value is expanded. A heart of compassion is revealed. A relationship is desired. A hearing is earned. Submission to another to learn is the foundation of conversation. Trust is built. There is absence of oppression and judgments in the atmosphere. Dr. Leonard Sweet makes clear the point that churches are a place for listeners.

> Communities of faith might better be called hearing rooms where God is given listening room. To hear the Gospels is to hear the voice of Christ, and with that hearing comes obedience.[14]

13. Dever, *What Is a Healthy Church*, 97.
14. Sweet, *Nudge*, 152.

As God listens patiently with us, so shall we with the broken hearted and downtrodden.

The theme of listening is God's model of interaction with the destitute.[15] We are to pay attention to the victims that have no voice on the earth. Scripture emphasizes that God's ears are attentive to the prayers of the voiceless. Outreach involves listening both as a spiritual discipline and in reaching out to the hurting. Listening is the start of discernment. There is also a practice of listening to the voiceless. God points people out that may need others to speak for them. God does this with us personally in the depths of our desperateness.[16]

Many times in ministry as a military chaplain, soldiers who had been hurt in the past would approach me with a "trial balloon," a surface counseling issue that was not the real issue or need they wanted to talk about. Most of the time, soldiers would watch you like a hawk, waiting and deciding if you were trustworthy or not with some of their deepest hurts or fears. This is not unlike Christians being watched in the workplace to see if they are "real" about their trust in God. A shame or regret is often eating someone alive from the inside out. You do not share that with just anyone. The world does not readily see the answer of Jesus Christ. Hurting individuals need the discerning Christian to lead them to a listening God.

Listening is to be done correctly with the right motivation. A ministry program that does not value the voiceless will use listening for self-gain in its program. Personal satisfaction or control is not godly ministry motivation. Geoff Gorsuch explains what can happen within the context of a small ministry group. He explains that there are three false listening practices that ministries can fall into. They are: (1) shallow listening—fake listening to promote our agenda later; (2) selective listening—focusing on our interests in order to control the conversation to our benefit; (3) self-protective listening to protect ourselves from messages perceived as a threat.[17]

15. Ps 10:14, 17–18.
16. Ps 102:19–20; Rom 8:26–27.
17. Gorsuch, *Brothers!*, 29–30.

He explains the movement from looking at listening as a task to the exhortation of Philippians 2:3–4:

> To listen well, we must remember that it is an attitude, not an activity. It is a sign that indicates our dependence upon God and one another in humility.[18]

In ministry to the hurting, the art of listening and speaking is in the context of confidentiality. The atmosphere of trust and safety will be a healing balm built by genuine listening on the wounds of the brokenness, violation, anger, and un-beckoned intrusion. What may seem obvious is actually a common error in the outreach of presence to the voiceless. Words are the surface of a broken heart that needs to be listened to. As stated before, sometimes a counselee will use words to cover the real pain inside them. Words, emotions, body language and the meaning under words are protection for those who have suffered greatly, and need listening discernment.

Spirit-filled Christians will show greater discernment with a consistent walk with Jesus Christ and more capacity to pray in all things. Prayer must go beyond the "sick list" often heard in our churches today. Prayer and discernment is a community effort. There were times in the military chaplaincy when I was at the end of my capability to help or discern a soldier's spiritual challenge before him or her. Only because of the prayers of a home church with faithful saints who held me up to the Lord could answers be discerned.

The Sound That God's Ears Are Especially Attuned To

In your local church ministry is there room for active listening? One's outreach lens is to include time and space for intentional listening. In our vision to reach the fatherless, do we match God's listening to the deep, unutterable, wounded voice of the hurting? It is my conviction as I read God's letter describing himself to us, that his ears are particularly sensitive to the sound of the innocent.

18. Ibid, 30.

Why would that be? God is sensitive to his Son's innocent sacrifice for sin and to those who plead complete dependence upon God's salvific power. From Abel's innocent, voiceless blood crying out to God, to the martyrs under his throne, God hears and is aroused by the voices of the innocent. He will act in absolute and complete vindication.[19] Unsolved murders, abortion, hidden human trafficking, unknown abused children, saints of God who have died unrecorded; all are seen and heard by God almighty.[20]

God is very specific as to what he hears. Several times in Scripture, God says he will hear the "cry" of the widow and orphan and it will cause him to be angry.[21] God expects his people to be a voice for the voiceless. We are to "plead" the cause of the fatherless.[22] Justice and vindication cannot be exerted for the powerless without intentional listening. Even a court does not administer justice without a great deal of listening with systematic checks and balances to get right and wrong facts defined and heard correctly.

Back to Presence

The ministry of presence is proven powerful in the ministry of the chaplaincy. In the depths of grief, the joys of completing a mission, the long road march with the troops, and the 2400 to 0100 (12 PM to 1 AM civilian time) visit to a faraway mountain top outpost in a Signal Unit. For the pastor or elder of a church it is the same; the valley of death, the new infant, graduations, walking with people through difficulties, and visiting the work places of faithful saints. Presence is a choice and not accidental. It is foundational to ministry opportunities and building bridges to the brokenhearted. Our "fatherless" outreach lens includes the power of presence, God's power in us.

---

19. Gen 4:10; Lk 23:41, Rev 6:9b–10.
20. Heb 4:12–13, emphasis on v. 13.
21. Exod 22:22-24; Job 29:12.
22. Jer 5:28b.

Leadership Study Questions

1. Do we create space for the presence of God in us within our local church?

2. Do we embody God's presence in our fellowship and outreach?

3. Does our church have a well-defined plan for the presence of God in our local church?

4. Do we have programs and methods that allow for presence?

5. Is God's priority of presence reflected in our missions, worship, and local church outreach?

6. Who is in need of the presence of God?

7. What are the elements needed to flesh out godly presence (time, commitment, initiation, determination, etc.)?

8. When does godly presence have the largest impact?

   "Religion that God our Father accepts as pure and faultless is this: to _____ _____ orphans and widows in their _____ and to keep oneself from being polluted by the world" (Jas 1:27).

9. Does faithful, godly presence before the time of a person's crisis help during a time of overwhelming pain (physically and emotionally)?

10. What is a good methodology to use when practicing the ministry of presence?

For Next Week

Read the next chapter.

- Read the "fatherless" passages.

- Pray for relationships to be seen as God defines it in your local church ministry.

- Identify your church's teaching (word and deed) on godly relationships.

9

Generational

If you really change your ways and your actions and deal with each
other justly, if you do not oppress the alien, the fatherless or the widow
and do not shed innocent blood in this place, and if you do not follow
other gods to your own harm, then I will let you live in this place, in
the land I gave your forefathers for ever and ever.

—JEREMIAH 7:5–7

His mercy extends to those who fear him, from generation to
generation.

—LUKE 1:50 (MARY'S SONG)

It is not hard to see that we are on a horrible course of fatherlessness in our present generation. Among children who were a part of
the "post-war generation," 87.7 percent grew up with two biologi-
cal parents who were married to each other. Today only 68.1 percent will spend their entire childhood in an intact family.[1] With
the increasing number of premarital births and a continuing high

---

1. See US Census Bureau, "Living Arrangements of Children."

divorce rate, the proportion of children living with just one parent rose from 9.1 percent in 1960 to 20.7 percent in 2012. Currently, 55.1 percent of all black children, 31.1 percent of all Hispanic children, and 20.7 of all white children are living in single-parent homes.[2] Then there is the quieter side of the statistics, fathers who are geographically separated because of war, medical illness including psychiatric needs, boarding schools, and abortions. All of these are contributing in some way to the care or lack of care in the next generation. God sees it all; he has said so.[3]

Sociologists and psychologists recognize the destructive nature to generations when there is a high rate of "fatherlessness." Wade Mackey and Ronald Immerman write,

> Without commenting upon desirability, it is argued that, when compared to alternative familial structures, those cultures which both minimize fatherless families and systematically restrict women's roles to that of motherhood do and will have—across generations—a demographic advantage. And, in terms of cultural evolution, i.e. across generations, those cultures which emphasize triadic families of father & mother & children are positioned to systematically displace and/or to replace those cultures which emphasize the mother & children dyadic family.[4]

While secular researchers decry the lack of evolutionary development of the traditional roles of family structure, it is recognized in statistical and generational facts that God's institution will remain a dominant norm.

Generational Sight

God's line of sight is generational. He cares about the generations to come. This speaks to a view of ministry that reaches beyond our lifetime and present knowledge. This was God's message to Jonah

2. Ibid.
3. Mal 3:5; Heb 4:13.
4. Mackey and Immerman, "Cultural Evolution," 155.

who was nursing his puny present day woes and biases.[5] God emphasized his compassion along with his justice to be visited to the fourth generation.[6] He also emphasized the follow through of his covenant promises to "1000" generations even to the revelation of the church.[7] Since we are not God, what is the practical outcome for us who do not see all the generations in eternity? Simply put, we are to do more than simply invest only for the here-and-now result in ministry.

Krista Petty writes for the Externally Focused Church Movement on how "statistics show that most social ills can be traced back to fatherlessness."[8] She further points out the generational commitment needed:

> But working with children, especially those in the community who may come and go out of the program, can be frustrating work. People don't always get involved because they do not see immediate results. You have to pour your life into kids and realize that you may never see the results.[9]

Doorways to Generational Sight

Traditions, affirmation, storytelling, remembering, testimony and the local church's story are all important handles in the practice of presenting godliness from generation to generation.

Traditions. Our society at large in America has put aside traditions. In the traditional military worship service the Lord's Prayer is recited.[10] Dr. Leonard Sax warns:

5. Jonah 4:11.

6. Exod 34:7.

7. Ps 105:8; Eph 3:21.

8. For an example of an externally focused church, see http://www.thevistacommunity.com/mission-vision.

9. Petty, "Fathering the Fatherless," 43.

10. Matt 6:9–13: "'This, then, is how you should pray: 'Our Father in heaven, hallowed be your name, your kingdom come, your will be done on earth as it is in heaven. Give us this day our daily bread. Forgive us our debts, as we

Think twice before you look condescendingly at the traditions of other cultures that have lasted far longer than our own. Our culture's neglect of the transition to manhood is not producing an overabundance of young men who are sensitive, caring, and hardworking. . . . We ignore the importance of these traditions at our peril.[11]

Affirmation. When one is tuned into the priorities of what God sees, there is less of a need to have affirmation for performing one's task and recognition of the lasting affirmation that comes from a personal relationship with God. Our affirmation is to bring glory to a God who is worthy of all creation's greatest ascriptions. We, like Christ, will pour ourselves out as a drink offering, energized by the loving heart of God and his power. It is God's glory and affirmation we seek.[12]

Storytelling. If the local church is generational in ministry, methodologies of storytelling and mentorship need to be practiced. Ministry allows those who have been saved to tell their story. Storytelling is crucial to spiritual development. My very intelligent grandson does not talk. Maybe my expectations are too high. He is only one and a half as of this writing. But he makes a lot of interesting noises and in doing so, communicates. His toys often talk to one another. They say things: noises, grunts, high-pitched squeals, with serious expressions and happy sounds. This unbiased grandpa knows for a fact that storytelling is going on. I share this because, as a church, we tend to like our polished and popular testimonies. There are a lot of stories to be told in a growing Christian's life.

---

also have forgiven our debtors. And lead us not into temptation, but deliver us from the evil one.'" Note: The military commonly adds, "For thine is the Glory forever and ever, Amen!" In the military this prayer is a tradition, a handle, a token, a familiar piece within the multitudes of worship methodologies of hundreds of denominations. The following is why it is done. A military man or woman will say to themselves, "I am in a place of worship," "I am home," "I recognize where I am at," "God will meet me here."

11. Sax, *Boys Adrift*, 171.

12. Note: Affirmation has a mistaken identity with flattery. Flattery is a falsehood. The practice of affirmation is a statement of that which is true and positive. If it is anything other than that, "silence is golden," as it is commonly said.

The words are not polished and often not theologically correct. Yet, they need to be told. If you are older, elderly, like me? Perhaps you remember the 1960s? Those stories were "far out, man!" But wise church leaders allowed time and space for infant Christians to tell about what God was doing in their lives. Many of those "immature" Christians a few decades back are now mature spiritual leaders.

Storytelling allows for declaration and builds up confidence. It is important to remember our "first love,"[13] salvation, or commitment to Christ. Multiple times after God told the children of Israel to pay attention to the widow, fatherless, and the stranger, he told them to "remember that you were slaves in Egypt, and follow carefully these decrees."[14]

Testimonies. A testimony is simply storytelling centered around what God has done through Jesus Christ. Fathers, boys, and men are generally visual. Stories captivate them. Storytelling/ testimonies are real, lived-out experiences that others can learn from. There is transformational power in both the listening and the telling of real-life wrestling with God. Soong-Chan Rah, associate professor at North Park Theological Seminary in Chicago, makes these societal observations concerning storytelling/testimonies,

> Aristotle stated, "When storytelling goes bad, the result is decadence." Society and culture cannot progress and be transformed without real, honest, and powerful stories. The church also loses its influence if it fails to engage in powerful storytelling.[15]

When one is willing to share and one is willing to listen to the messiness of one's life, a powerful dynamic of transference of cleansing, affirming, resolution, reaffirming, recommitment, truth telling, recognition, etc. contributes to the wellness of the community of faith. Soong-Chan Rah explains further the experience of what transfers into his life through the telling of a story:

13. Rev 2:4.
14. Deut 16:12.
15. Rah, *Many Colors*, 130.

To hear of someone who has overcome so many obstacles encourages me to face the obstacles that I have experienced in my own life story. His willingness to speak of his pain and struggle emboldens me to share the stories of my pain and struggle. His ability to rise above the struggle and speak a strong prophetic word encourages me to rise above and speak the truth, no matter what the obstacles.[16]

As the children of Israel, "it is our reasonable service"[17] to reach out to the fatherless because God reached out to us.[18] God wants us to remember our salvation and make that a motivating factor for reaching out to the fatherless. Remembering God's salvation is to be a practice and motivation to reach the broken.[19] It is a command of God throughout Scripture and it is found in sharing our story of good news.

Lay leader training in churches needs to include what we used to call "testimony." It is much more than telling of one's salvation experience. When one tells of pivotal events that Christ caused in his/her life and telling of failure or victory in reaching out, it is a dynamic of "iron sharpening iron,"[20] lending strength to another doing the unknown, and modeling generationally what "right" looks like. Descriptions of pain and solutions to it, finding different choices of words and different emotional expressions, and the spiritual growth of the person telling the story of God's strength and love are opportunities that many church bodies are currently missing. We work hard to get "high-powered" speakers at great expense. All the while changed lives are in our midst, and God has guided them through a mess or a victory in a special way

16. Ibid., 144.

17. Rom 12:1.

18. Rom 5:8.

19. Note: Remembering is an often-commanded exhortation in the Bible. Joshua 4—The children of Israel with the twelve stones to remember the crossing into the promised land. First Samuel 17—David remembered that God delivered the lion and the bear into his hand before going against Goliath. Even greater things happened with the people of God who "remembered."

20. Prov 27:17.

for a purpose; let it be told. Our "fatherless" outreach lens needs to include generational storytelling.

Local Church Story. Tom Berlin is a pastor, and Lovett Weems Jr. is the director of the Lewis Center for Church Leadership at Wesley Theological Seminary, in Washington, DC, emphasizing the importance of a local church's story. Along with individual stories there is also a collective community fellowship's story.

> The good news is that the congregation's own story and values can often act as a lever for change. People typically honor the history of their congregation and want to see the church be consistent with its heritage. Knowing the congregation's story, leaders can remind the congregation of the very best of its history and how these qualities can be lived out today. New members also benefit from hearing the story. It acts as a portal through which they step into community.[21]

Storytelling from individuals of faith or local churches can pass on God's values from generation to generation. Philip Hearne and Gary Blackmon's music emphasize the importance of passing on a godly influence in a storytelling song called "Lonely Sunday."

> A tractor sits lonely out on a hill; the fields have grown up not plowed in some years.
>
> Things taken for granted have now disappeared.
>
> We miss the old folks, do you miss those years?
>
> What are we gonna do when the old folks are gone?
>
> No more Sunday dinners, we feel so alone, who'll set the table who'll say the grace
>
> Precious old memories now take their place.
>
>
> If you look at your life and the things left behind, will they still remember in the back of their minds, your life on this earth will soon pass you by?

---

21. Berlin and Weems, "Lever for Change," 10–11.

You only get one chance to leave it behind. What are we gonna do when the old folks are gone? No more Sunday dinners, we feel so alone. Who'll set the table, who'll say the grace? Precious old memories now take their place.

Chorus:

Now she'll set the table, now he'll say the grace, the next generation has taken their place.[22]

Let us pass on the story of Jesus Christ and God's abundant grace through storytelling, traditions, affirmations, testimony, song, and discipleship.

My dad experienced the loss of a father, the loss of a mother to a mental institution, put up for adoption, and a life of constantly moving from place to place. He thirsted for a stable family; he found that it was a possibility with God. He looked to possibly minimize the loss that he experienced in his sons. He started a tradition of naming his sons should the worst happen. My dad, David Wyatt Croy, named me Dwight David Croy and my brother, Stephen Wyatt Croy. We in turn have named our sons Wyatt John Croy and Jonathan Dwight Croy. This is called connection. Knowing where one comes from and knowing where one is going is a generational value. I am thankful for a dad who saw generationally for his family and also in the ministry of the local church.

God's vision is generational. It is telescopic in nature, looking down through the ages ahead of us. The generations that matter, sit among our congregations. Are the ministries of our local churches seeing past their lifetime? We often desire to minister where we will be able to see results. God wants us to depend on his vision for ministry that sees into eternity. Our outreach lens must include influencing the generations.

---

22. Written by Philip Hearne and Gary Blackmon, ©2004.

Leadership Study Questions

1. Do we have a generational influence in our outreach ministry within our local church?

2. Do we minister with a generational lens of ministry?

   "His mercy extends to those who fear him, from _____ to _____" (Luke 1:50).

3. Does our church have a generational plan of ministry; will it bear fruit beyond your lifetime?

4. Do we have programs and methods that allow for generational ministry?

5. Is God's view of generations reflected in our missions, worship, and local church outreach?

6. Why is a generational view of ministry important to God; to the destitute?

7. What are the elements needed to flesh out a generational outreach (time, commitment, initiation, determination, etc.)?

8. Do we need to see the result of our ministry efforts? Is there a place for measurement and evaluation? Is there a place for working hard in ministry and not seeing the results right away?

9. What is a good methodology to use when emphasizing generational ministry?

For Next Week

Read the next chapter.

- Read the "fatherless" passages.

- Pray for your church to see beyond the present generation and ask God for visionary goals in your local church that will last past your lifetime.

- Identify ministries in your church that are generational in nature, bolster them and make certain that they are resourced.

10

Justice

Cursed is the man who withholds justice from the alien, the fatherless or the widow. Then all the people shall say, "Amen!"

—DEUTERONOMY 27:19

Woe to you Pharisees, because you give God a tenth of your mint, rue and all other kinds of garden herbs, but you neglect justice and the love of God. You should have practiced the latter without leaving the former undone.

—LUKE 11:42

In our forty-three "fatherless" Scripture passages, there is more reference to justice than any other factor. If there is a passage that should send a chill down our nation's backs, it is Deuteronomy 27. Within this passage we have a direct reference to justice being withheld from the alien, the fatherless, and the widows.[1] After reading such a passage, our depraved minds reason, "Well, we have not done all these bad things, just some of them." Or, "We only

1. Deut 27:19

have done some of these thingshalf-way as a nation " Such is the state of our depravity, straddling the sins of commission and the sins of omission, dwelling in the state of reasoning that assuages the guilt of our trespasses.

This issue of justice in our "fatherless" lens will test our resolve in exercising true compassion. Justice is often out of the reach of the defenseless. The poor and destitute lack money, reputation, a name or lineage, and opportunity to reach for their own justice; their greatest need is for someone to step up and put their own means, courage, name, and reputation on the line. Judgment, or *din* in Hebrew, is a justice needed on behalf of another.

In the verses related to the fatherless, vindication is prayed for on behalf of the downtrodden.[2] A perfect vindication like revenge can only come from an absolute authoritative creator.[3] God will manage his own glory. Yet, God has told us repetitively to "plead the cause," "defend," and "do justice."[4] These phrases are examples of vindication in Scripture. These are ours to do within the stewardship of God's power. God expects his created peoples to steward justice on behalf of the destitute who are taken advantage of by world systems that do not have a foundation of God's sacrifice as their motivation. Dr. Ken Wytsma, president of Kilns College, explains the balance.

> God's plan of salvation and restoration, both temporally and finally, are organically connected to the restoration and institution of justice. Justice cannot be divorced from God's heart and purposes—it permeates them. In fact, a central truth of the gospel is this: God's grace enacts and restores justice.[5]

True vindication is not done by a world system that has no view to the inherent value God places on his creation. Creation should ultimately bring glory to God. A local church that becomes

---

2. Ps 82:3; Ps 94:6–7.
3. Deut 32:35; Heb 10:30-31.
4. Deut 24:17; Jer 5:28; 22:3; Zech 7:10.
5. Wytsma, "Pursuing Justice," 41–42.

a world system and not representative of "blood-bought" and "peculiar" people will lose its way and God will remove its light (God-ordained effectiveness). The saints of God have an empathetic understanding of what it took for God to save mankind. The saints of God are best suited to represent the justice of God as he has commanded us. Vindication is the action of "doing justice" and restoring the downtrodden person.

In order to fully grasp justice for the fatherless, violence must be defined first. Violence is an unchecked and unauthoritative action that harms people made in the image of God. Violence is wrongly ascribed to a nation at war. War is a sanctioned, law-restricted, and national stewardship of power, weighed, discussed, and written down, with delegated plans of action, with no one person's personal agenda at stake. Following the same logic, a state is not doing violence to a person sentenced to die on death row. Laws, courts, juries, and a complete justice system are put in place to bring safety, security, and peace to a law-abiding land. On the other hand, when a person acts on his or her own with no authority for one's action and harms another person or persons because of one's own self-interest, deranged or premeditated designs, this indeed is rightly called violence.

God is perfect justice. As created beings, therefore, we cannot design our own parameters, but rather need to fall in line with his definitions. When it comes to a filter of justice in the paradigm of ministry outreach, the church is to invest in a very visible and public "take a stand" approach. America is one of the top giving nations in the world in money and social concern. But to give in the area of justice is to give with one's reputation and standing in the community. To exercise justice is to put one's name and reputation on the line and is, frankly, a more frontal approach to the world. We must ask ourselves; do we dare to publically challenge injustice with abandon?

Justice as an element of outreach is often not within our mission or scope of vision. Thank God for the many saints who go before our court systems to stand up for and with the abused, divorced, orphaned, etc. Thank God for those who spend time with petitions that represent God's heart.

If the church is committed to helping in the muck and mire of this world, we cannot ignore also the contrary actions of those already fatherless. Working with juvenile teenagers, it is easy to see that violence can have its way among the fatherless. Tough love and justice can be inserted into the depravity already exhibited. As a chaplain and a pastor, one has an opportunity to speak to the command or the courts on behalf of a struggling youth. The church is to stand for justice in this sense as well; to be a support, an eye witness to recent personal change, and standing with young people in the thick of their storm. In 1995, Paul McNulty warned of the coming storm of violence that has since arrived in America:

> More violent crime is committed by older teenagers than by any other age group. Teenagers from fatherless homes commit more crime than teenagers from intact families. Put these two demographic facts together, and we are in for a catastrophe in the early 21st century.[6]

Of course the church's desire is to reach the "fatherless" before they self-destruct, but we are to intentionally walk in grace with the individual until the point of no return, which is God's call, not ours.

But there is more to do as a body of believers as well. Laws can be addressed. Injustice can be addressed. Opposing groups with large amounts of money, law, physical attacks, and the court of public opinion, these groups are systematically working to destroy family base support systems that reach out to the fatherless. Churches who reach out to at-risk youth along with Boy Scouts of America, Kentucky Baptist Homes for Children (KBHC), and Big Brothers and Big Sisters are the battleground of the homosexual issue. There are systematic efforts against family support systems and a complacency that is caustic to our national future. Simply, we have allowed godly institutions to be dismantled by the

---

6. McNulty, "Natural Born Killers," 84–85.

selfish.[7] Alan Sears, president and CEO of the Alliance Defense Fund, along with Craig Osten, the vice-president, are influencing the court systems for Christ. They state the following:

> When local governments evict the Scouts, these boys lose the moral guidance and life skills they so desperately need. However, in the view of homosexual activists and their allies it is more important in some cases, to move the homosexual agenda forward than to save troubled boys.[8]

This concerted effort shows a depraved end-state to the general public. God has already warned us about our judgment if we do not take care of the fatherless. The reason we do not do these things is that we are afraid of derailment. Politics, media, and other scary things can get the church off track from its mission of the great commission. The common mantra of not mixing politics with religion has rendered many Christians impotent; at minimum silent. Plus, it is plain old hard, unpleasant, and thankless work. However, if the pursuit is principled justice on behalf of the powerless, it will remain a godly priority. Robert Lupton, the director of Family Consultation Service Urban Ministries, envisions the future placement of compassionate justice.

> *Gentrification is our new reality.* Some rail against it; others laud its arrival. But for good or for ill, it is our new reality, and it will only increase in the years to come. Gentrification means to welcome new economic and social life for our cities and, with the proactive involvement of the saints, can introduce a whole new era of hopefulness to the poor. Our mantra must be: gentrification with justice.[9]

---

7. Sears and Osten, *Homosexual Agenda*, 193–96.

8. Ibid., 191.

9. Lupton, *Compassion, Justice and the Christian Life*, 119. Gentrification: "The upgrading of run-down urban neighborhoods by affluent people who buy and renovate the properties, thereby displacing the resident poor" (*Random House Webster's College Dictionary*, s.v., "gentrification").

Pure justice is unattainable by the created. As much as we try, it is beyond our grasp. To act justly is folded into walking humbly with our God.[10] According to Scripture, "to act justly is not optional. It is a part of what is good. Justice is a part of our outreach lens.

We must not align with the secular world's end state of utopia. Our false religious bent often gets us on a trail of spiritual utopia. Some churches want to be the compassion comfort cocoon that snuggles up and shares a vision of God's love without explaining the gritty ramifications of that costly love. God wants us to bring restoration, healing, and relationships of deep satisfaction to the brokenhearted. This requires us to be representatives (ambassadors) of our King (Jesus Christ) in the eternal dwelling to come.

When speaking of justice in the Word of God, "defense" is a major principle. Nothing motivates a United States soldier more that defending the weak and powerless. In Scripture we see that God is a defender of the weak, poor, and fatherless.[11] This is the action of vindication that we see in the Psalms. Do we reflect this part of God? In the military we would paraphrase personal defending of one "stepping up" or "having one's back." Orphans are so vulnerable, who has their backs? Johnny Carr, an advocate of orphans, sheds light to the global epidemic of misplaced children:

> The 153 million orphaned and vulnerable children worldwide guarantee a continued market from which human traffickers can draw. For children living outside of families, no one will ever know they're missing. There is no moral outcry, no legal search, and likely no one who even cares.[12]

Scripture is clear, we are to look around us and defend those near us. If you do not see someone at risk in your area of influence, you may not be seeing as God sees. Carr provides a wider but closer-to-home view on human trafficking:

10. Mic 6:8.

11. Ps 68:5–6; Ps 82:3–4.

12. Carr, *Orphan Justice*, 24.

In all likelihood, trafficking is happening right now in your community. Consider ways that your congregation can reach out to and build relationships with at-risk children in your church, area schools, and community. Become a foster parent. Mentor at-risk kids. Host an after-school program. Start a basketball league. Seek out and build relationships with kids in your youth program whose parents are incarcerated or absent. Take a preemptive strike at trafficking in your community by ensuring that vulnerable youth have a safe place and a support system to turn to.[13]

We are to take God's command seriously to take care of the fatherless, widow, and disconnected.[14] He expects our salvation to be worked out in this way.[15]

Justice not only represents defense, but also security and safety. Long after my being an adult, I found out that my dad would often look in on me during my elementary school years. A true father defends. One time in first grade, my dad found out that I was being bullied and one day my coat was taken by the bullies. This is a big deal for a couple of reasons: (1) we lived in Astoria, Oregon, and it was a cold, wet place, and (2) a preacher's salary is not very big sometimes. A coat could set you back a few shekels. To my first-grade eyes, my dad came out like a lion and talked to the bullies back in the day when you could actually put the fear of God into someone without being arrested. This involved a one-way conversation, elevated voice, red face, and some hand motions. In Astoria, everything is on a hill including your front yard. Dad used

13. Ibid., 32.

14. Note: In ministry it could be as simple as standing with someone who needs to tell the truth to an ominous authority figure. For example, marriage counseling or standing with soldiers as they communicate with individuals in their chain of command. Still others need to lovingly confront a church or family member with someone strong in faith nearby. Praying with someone who is going into surgery or going with someone who needs to forgive a person who does not comprehend forgiveness are more examples of bringing about justice through defending.

15. Phil 2:12. Note: This exhortation is in the context of unity in the body of Christ.

this high ground to his advantage and gave a Jericho shout before he brought a passionate education to these neighborhood children. But I always remember that I felt protected and safe, because I had my secret weapon, my dad. My dad taught me about God in that way. The fatherless or the lonely need someone to show them God by being a protection.

Justice provides a sanctuary or a "city of refuge" when life is confusing and in turmoil.[16] A young soldier with posttraumatic stress came to our "Soldiers' Chapel" in Anchorage, Alaska, and became agitated when a child started to cry. An alert chaplain assistant escorted the young man, who had no church background and no concept of God or his love, to a chaplain, where he was listened to and helped. The soldier was ignorant of the term "sanctuary" in connecting to our Father God, but was seeking out its experience for his life. He came to know only one focus . . . Go to the chapel; someone knows God there. Sit in the sanctuary; help is there. Beyond our churches being a "sanctuary," do we have first responders in our assemblies that represent in their person the "sanctuary" that God the Father represents?

There is a lasting feeling of being secure in a father's arms. As a child I loved to sit on my father's lap and listen to him speak with my ear up to his chest. The deep vibrating sounds were more than a unique sound that I had found. The experience of sitting in my father's lap was a place of safety, comfort, strength, and love. The smell of my dad's aftershave and the predictable way he talked or laughed were representative of security and safety. Anthony J. Showalter captured this feeling we have with God when ministering to grieving friends with Deuteronomy 33:27a. He then wrote "Leaning on the Everlasting Arms."[17] John Eldredge, a needed

16. Num 35:11. Note: six cities of refuge, three on each side of the Jordan for those who accidently killed someone (manslaughter, in today's terms).

17. Osbeck, *Amazing Grace*, 85. *What a fellowship, what a joy divine, leaning on the everlasting arms; What a blessedness, what a peace is mine, leaning on the everlasting arms. O how sweet to walk in this pilgrim way, leaning on the everlasting arms; O how bright the path grows from day to day, leaning on the everlasting arms. What have I to dread, what have I to fear, leaning on the everlasting arms? I have blessed peace with my Lord so near, leaning on the*

voice for unapologetic masculinity, also shares the need for a world that is safe:

> The safety that a father's strength provides and allows a boy to be a boy, creates the universe for a boy's heart to come fully alive. . . . When a boy has this confidence, this security and safety created by a masculine strength over him, the whole world opens before him. He is able to live *as a boy*—an explorer and adventurer.[18]

More and more in today's sick and depraved world, our outreach and ministry is to be a place of transparency and excellence in safety.

Those who are blessed with the security of a protective and loving father have a hard time comprehending or imagining that a person out in the world does not have a single person or place of security. We as the "body of Christ" are to help establish a person and give them a "handle" of strength and security. Many well-intentioned organizations give to the disenfranchised, only for them to be dependent on the outreach organizations' resources. This is not the experience of security or sanctuary where needs are met. Communication of the safety of our Father, God, is a needed message. Role models of safe fathers are needed. An atmosphere of safety and accountability in our faith communities and physical buildings will be the heavenly touch deeply hurting people need. Before we focus on the world's depravity, we desire to put our own house in order. In light of a horrific and terrifying world, lying in its shadow is the depravity in ecclesiastical leadership; churches would do well to review policies and procedures to mitigate internal misconduct. Clergy, volunteers, and attendees at church are to feel a presence of safety. Linda Oxford is a Tennessee Supreme Court Rule 31 Listed Mediator and has over thirty years of experience as a therapist, trainer, educator, and consultant in the public and private sectors. She states:

---

everlasting arms. Chorus: Leaning, leaning, safe and secure from all alarms; leaning, leaning, leaning on the everlasting arms.

18. Eldredge, *Fathered by God*, 42–43.

Preventing clergy sexual misconduct and protecting vulnerable others require ongoing attention and activity on the part of church leaders and a capacity by leaders to effectively respond to present conditions and needs. Church leaders who focus their efforts on the primary prevention of misconduct, which involves efforts to avoid misconduct before it occurs, tend to be the most effective. Prevention of clergy misconduct requires visionary rather than reactive leadership, and efforts by the congregation are unlikely to be successful unless the leadership fully supports and leads the change effort.[19]

Our ministry outreach filter includes quantifiable security within the body life of a church, its facilities, and outreach relationship to its community.

Some might argue that creating a safe environment is not the "work of the ministry." In today's world, I would argue that it is an attractor and not a detractor. Greater is a parent's worship, knowing that their child is in a safe nursery. Greater is the attraction of the abused when they see visionary leadership go to great effort to provide a safe and secure Christian worship, evangelism, education, and communion environment. A leadership's stewardship of safety and security is a large part of justice.

Let us not just seethe with righteous indignation at the injustice in the world, let us put our being, our "living sacrifice,"[20] into the battle fray and exercise justice for the powerless. Justice is a needed lens to see the "fatherless" of our world.

---

19. Oxford, "What Healthy Churches Do," 107.

20. Rom 12:1–2.

Leadership Study Questions

1. Do we have a justice lens in our outreach ministry within our local church?

   "'Cursed is the man who withholds _____ from the alien, the fatherless or the widow.' Then all the people said, 'Amen!'" (Deut 27:19).

2. Do we have programs and methods that allow for justice in ministry?

3. Is God's view of justice reflected in our missions, worship, and local church outreach?

4. Why is a justice view of ministry important to God; to the destitute?

5. What are the elements needed to flesh out justice in outreach (time, commitment, initiation, determination, reputation, etc.)?

6. Do we defend, vindicate, or show courage on behalf of the destitute?

7. What is a good methodology to use when emphasizing justice in ministry? Are we concerned about the safety and security of worship along with other outreach programs? Are we a sanctuary personally and as a church body? Are we passive about injustice in our local area (corporately or individually)?

8. Are we a voice for the voiceless? What does that look like? (Voting, community volunteering, visiting the bedridden, checks and balances for looking after children, going to court for support of someone who has made bad choices, mentoring someone in prison.)

For Next Week

Read the next chapter.

- Read the "fatherless" passages.

- Pray for your church to flesh out justice in its local ministry.

- Identify ministries in your church that are concerned with justice, bolster them and make certain that they are resourced.

11

Dignity / God-Worth

Their evil deeds have no limit; they do not plead the case of the fatherless to win it, they do not defend the rights of the poor.

—JEREMIAH 5:28B

My brothers, as believers in our glorious LORD Jesus Christ, don't
show favoritism.

—JAMES 2:1

God-worth, not self-worth, is how we are to treat all individuals.
This is another way of affirming the image of God in all peoples and
their groupings. The Hebrew way of helping the poor was handed
down by God. Most of the fatherless Scripture passages in Exodus
and Deuteronomy are followed up with a program of helping the
widow, fatherless, and alien by a system that contained both work
and charity. Old Testament directives concerning the poor further
expected a connection and an invitation to be included in major
community events, celebration and holy days.

It is amazing that our compassionate governmental, ecclesiastical and nonprofit charitable efforts often extinguish the fire of dignity and self-worth in people. There are two kinds of people in poverty and want. Dr. Ruby Payne, who is a leading expert on poverty mindsets, comments:

> Generational poverty has its own culture, hidden rules, and belief systems. One of the key indicators of whether it is generational or situational poverty is the prevailing attitude. Often the attitude in generational poverty is that society owes one a living. In situational poverty the attitude is often one of pride and a refusal to accept charity. Individuals in situational poverty often bring more resources with them to the situation than those in generational poverty.[1]

In this quote we see how crucial it is not to let the destitute languish without meeting their needs and providing an avenue for them to meet those needs on their own.

Real Balance Not a Balancing Act

God charges us to not only meet their need but to point out worth, build up, value, and affirm the image of God in all people—yes, even those who have no desire to exist or be around other people. The church is the only agency that can give with hope. Often we shortchange ourselves in our great commission and *only* give charity or *only* give a message of hope. They are to go hand in hand.[2] It is dangerous to the destitute to meet needs without giving a person the "fullness of life." The principle in Jeremiah 5:28b is to give more than a surface answer or meet more than a surface need. Dr. Wess Stafford, president and CEO of Compassion International, explains the danger of the church not reaching out in a correct fashion:

1. Payne, *Framework for Understanding Poverty*, 47.

2. Jas 2:14–17. A basic teaching of Scripture to show faith and works together; both prove the desire of God together.

Unless there is an intervention of love and hope, these seeds of apathy lead inevitably downward to an even lower death sentence called fatalism. The very word stinks of death. It is the bottom—as low as a human being can sink. When the human spirit becomes truly fatalistic, it is almost impossible to retrieve. This is complete and utter poverty, the end of the road.[3]

It is hard to comprehend sometimes in our Western mindset, but giving can take away the value of a person unless we rethink how we give.

In the midst of overwhelming want, we often meet one need, only to ignore another. The olives, grain, and grapes were left for the poor, and they themselves were to work and gather for their own food.[4] If a poor, slave, alien, widow, or orphan needed to eat, there was provision; however, there were no handouts because it was "one for all and all for one," a community was to see each other made in the valuable image of God. The work of your hands was considered something to be proud of. This concept does not have to be historically far away as noted by Robert Lupton in his book titled *Compassion, Justice and the Christian Life: Rethinking Ministry to the Poor*:

> A food co-op owned and operated by the poor is certainly superior to a free lunch program, both in dignity and responsibility. A co-op, through the mutual efforts of participants, expands the food dollars of those whose incomes are meager.[5]

Dignity as a value, in our outreach lens, is a start. Within each component of ministry focus there needs to be some soul searching. A drive to be comfortable and no longer reminded of pain, messiness, and want is to be replaced by wading into the uncomfortable. Robert Lupton again drives us toward harder thinking:

---

3. Stafford, *Too Small to Ignore*, 185.

4. Deut 24:19–22 emphasizes that the poor worked for what they ate.

5. Lupton, *Compassion, Justice and the Christian Life*, 54.

When our one-way giving becomes comfortable and our spirits are no longer stirred to find the deeper, more costly solutions, good has become the enemy of best. When our feeding programs value order and efficiency over the messiness of personal involvement, good has become the enemy of the best. When recipients remain recipients and givers are content to remain givers, good has become the enemy of best.[6]

Dignity or Bust

As noted before, those who do not understand compassion give with wrong motivation, value judgments, comparisons, and intentions. The Hebrew system was in place to maintain the dignity of those made in God's image. Part of the problem in standing up for the worth of an individual is that one often will stand alone (even in Christian community) in seeing the individual as God sees them. Brennan Manning describes the struggle.

> Anyone who has ever stood up for the truth of human dignity, no matter how disfigured, only to find previously supportive friends holding back, even remonstrating with you for your boldness, feels the loneliness of the poverty of uniqueness. This happens every day to those who choose to suffer for the absolute voice of conscience, even in what seem to be small matters. They find themselves standing alone. I have yet to meet the man or woman who enjoys such responsibility.[7]

If our outreach is for us to feel our value, it is not godly seed. If we reach out to maintain the value of the individual and indeed see them as the same as us, then we are closer to seeing as God sees. Our brokenness, sin, and shame are just as bad as anyone else's. If we find ourselves debating that, then we are currently incapable of a divine outreach and have fallen short in reaching out to the disenfranchised as God intended.

6. Ibid., 55.
7. Manning, *Abba's Child*, 137.

A person who treats others with God-worth does not accept society's norms and mores. You will know that you are victorious in this area when people look to you in shock because you invited them, included them, and addressed them with the conviction that they are as equally valuable to you as to God. There are a great many who have willfully devalued their own personhood. They are in need of a godly person to heal them with the actions and words of Jesus Christ.

Our lens of "fatherlessness" also includes dignity and respect. If we are to give dignity and worth to an individual, what would that look like right now? There are food programs that are controlled to the point of taking away dignity. For example: a person in charge hovering around the person as they shop to scrutinize the choices; a person in need may suffer the indignity of going through a checklist of requirements before help is given; food given indiscriminately; and pictures taken to promote the "success" of the program. Perhaps the best way to explain it is conditional love. Some of these things are governmental or donor requirements. Is our outreach embarrassing the *imago Dei?* As James says, do we have special seats for different kind of people?[8] God-worth is to be seen in every person that crosses our path without demotion or elevation.

8. Jas 2:1.

Leadership Study Questions

1. Do we see "God-worth" in our lens for ministry?

   "Their evil deeds have no limit; they do not plead the case of the fatherless to _____ it, they do not defend the rights of the poor" (Jer 5:28b).

2. Do we have programs and methods that allow for "God-worth" in ministry?

3. Is "God-worth" reflected in our missions, worship, and local church outreach?

4. Why is a "God-worth" view of ministry important to God; to the destitute?

5. What are the elements needed to flesh out "God-worth" in outreach (time, commitment, initiation, change in thinking or viewpoint, wording, etc.)?

6. How do we look at the destitute?

7. Are we comfortable in our categories? Are our levels and categories godly?

8. What is a good methodology to use when emphasizing "God-worth" in ministry? Do we all feel the same sense of "God-worth" personally and as a church body?

9. Are we putting "God-worth" into the disenfranchised or are we busy keeping them there?

10. What does God's position look like? What does his lens say to do?

For Weeks to Follow

Read the "fatherless" passages.

- Pray for your church to flesh out "God-worth" in your local ministry.

- Pray over God's direction for your church to insert God's "fatherless" principles into your local situation.

- Always pray to see God's heart in outreach and discipleship.

- Pray for a change in your own heart to match the heart of God. Write down an action that God has put on your heart with guidance of the Holy Spirit that is a positive directive to help your local church in. In the coming weeks I will _____

_____

_____

_____

_____

with God's strength and direction.

12

Conclusion: Comforted by God's Sight

The name of the LORD is a strong tower; the righteous run to it and
are safe.

—PROVERBS 18:10

The LORD is my rock, my fortress and my deliverer; my God is my
rock, in whom I take refuge.

—PSALM 18:2A

As a soldier, a strong tower is a good thing. It can be a very comforting thing on the battlefield. My son Jonathan and I have spent
time in towers for different reasons. He, being in the infantry, did
his time as a guard. I, as a chaplain, spent time with troops who
spent long hours on guard duty; so other soldiers could get their
rest and other missions done. God is our strong tower. There are
a lot of moving pieces on a battlefield. When you are a soldier,
you trust your generals and command leadership. It is a wonderful
thing to be a Christian soldier because you put your trust in God
who can see everything. It is also a great thing as a father and dad

to put your trust in God for the welfare of your family and especially when your son is in the same theater of operations.

We Are Not in Control

There are certain things on the human battlefield that generals cannot control, such as when and where a mortar will hit and when an IED (Improvised Exploding Device) will go off. Many soldiers walked or drove across some that would go off later. Red Cross messages concerning a family member at home is also another uncontrollable factor. Diseases, depression, post-traumatic stress are other impacts on the human battlefield. On the battlefield, it is unfathomable why some live and others die. For survivors, this brought about a very real human torment. Then there were mechanical devices breaking down. Every time I boarded a helicopter, I found that it was a good time for prayer.

God Is in Control

When we do ministry in the world, we are close to the ground unless we trust in the LORD. As a soldier you spend a lot of time facedown in the dirt, marching through dirt and gravel, and in the case of Iraq and Afghanistan, you eat a lot of dirt. You trust that somebody has the big picture. In giving the good news of the gospel out to the world, it is the same kind of mission. However, with God it is totally different than the limited sight of earthly generals. With God, he sees absolutely everything. Without sounding all "crystal ball" on you, he alone is the Great Seer. His perspective is higher, eternal, clear, and distinct. Yes, you can get all that from that "strong tower" verse. This should comfort us. Keeping this in mind makes the Christian life lighter and not burdensome. God repeatedly reminds us of his supreme perspective from Scripture.

Unlike generals who cannot see everything, we can march into the spiritual battlefield with confidence. We are more than conquerors because we are led by Jesus Christ.[1] When we come up with excuses, remember our fears, and spiritualize our earthly responses, like, "that's not my gift," we are not living in the strength of our Lord and Savior, Jesus Christ. He is the General.

Just Be Ready

As a soldier, you are thrust into the discipline and monotony of training for the day of the battle. You learn to low crawl through mud, and in my case, the sands of Fort Dix, New Jersey. Both my son Jonathan and I have now endured the sandstorms of Iraq and Kuwait. Anyone in the military can tell you of waiting in lines for supplies, food, shooting ranges, convoys, road marches, physical training, and medical inoculations. All are for the day of crisis or battle. As a Christian we faithfully pray, study and listen to the Word of God, to be ready for that specific interaction to which God has called us.[2]

We Have the Answers because of Jesus Christ

God has pointed us to the darkest areas of the world with the Old Testament triad of the alien, the fatherless, and the widow. The previous chapters were presented to help promote dialogue and finesse a focused mission for your local church. Truth lived out is often found by the intersection of crises in this world and Jesus Christ's great commission to us as ambassadors from an eternal heaven. The world's darkest problems are best addressed by Christians with eternal resources. The bare and uncovered problems as God defines them are void of worldly answers. In order to be victorious, we are to flee the comfortable and enter into the battle fray.

At this writing, God has moved me from the military crisis ministry to a juvenile boy's residential home ministry. Both have allowed me to minister in the area of crisis and both have allowed

1. Rom 8:37.
2. 1 Tim 4:2.

me to continue to influence the next generation for the LORD. Prayer and strength are needed. In the midst of such crisis ministry, it is easy to fall into a kind of gloomy feeling that you are alone in such efforts. The ministry God has called you and me to has within itself a kind of "encouragement" energy, a sweet spot of "knowing" you are exactly where God wants you to be. Remember God's word picture of the strong tower from the enemy.

Be Ready for Anything

A story I have shared from the pulpit many times comes from my Bible school days at Multnomah University, which was called at the time Multnomah School of the Bible. We had witnessing days where we would go out and tell people the good news of Jesus Christ. These were great teaching experiences and a foreshadowing of ministry to come. Many lessons came from these experiences, but one stands out in particular.

We went as a group, and at the time our team was made up of two women and two men. We would pray, obtain helpful literature, get our Bibles and split up into teams. It was not unusual to be nervous and wonder how we would approach people on the street. One of the girls with us approached two women at a bus stop and opened with, "Pardon me, do you know that you are sinners and are in danger of going to hell?" Since I am the son of a preacher, I sort of knew that something was amiss with this opening. My "common sense" approach told me that this might not end well for us. But guess what? God taught me something about willing obedience, the power of the Holy Spirit, and his desire to use what we have.

Yes, one response was exactly as expected. One lady stormed off, after a cursing tirade. The other did not follow in the same fashion, but turned to the young woman and said, "You know, hell has always bothered me, and I have always wanted to know how to stay away from hell." That very day, the young lady led a person to Christ with one of the "poorest" opening lines in witnessing history. Or was it? God, who fed the five thousand with a small step of obedience, a small gift, and willingness, taught a "know-all-about-it" preacher's son something more about himself, grew our whole team up in the obedience of witnessing, instilled confidence in a nervous witness, answered prayer, and planted a seed in another person.[3]

God Will Use You in a Mighty Way

The ripples and reverberations through eternity are made up of many unseen obedient saints of God. We often get enthralled with what we perceive as a moving of God on earth because we can see it physically in some way. God is a strong tower. In the spiritual battlefield, he sees the great and small in man's eyes; conversely, he sees the great and the small in his eyes. What God sees is what counts. God sees the "fatherless." What God focuses on tells us of his heart. Look at what God focuses on and be willing to move on his command. You have a strong tower telling you where to move and where to be an influence for Jesus Christ. God is always leading us to a perspective that is higher than us; moving us up a rocky mountain to see a panoramic view of the challenges and the glory that lie ahead of us. Be confident in your mighty God. He will use you in ways beyond your comprehension in the power of the Holy Spirit.

3. John 6:1–13.

Bibliography

Alden, Robert L. *Proverbs: A Commentary on an Ancient Book of Timeless Advice.* Grand Rapids: Baker, 1983.

Bayse, Daniel J. *Helping Hands: A Handbook for Volunteers in Prisons and Jails.* Upper Marlboro, MD: Graphic Communications, 1993.

Bennett, Daniel. *A Passion for the Fatherless: Developing a God-Centered Ministry to Orphans.* Grand Rapids: Kregel, 2011.

Berlin, Tom, and Lovett H. Weems, Jr. "A Lever for Change: Telling the Congregation's Story." *Christian Century,* April 19, 2011, 10–11.

Blackaby, Henry T., and Richard Blackaby. *Spiritual Leadership: Moving People on to God's Agenda.* Nashville: Broadman & Holman, 2011.

Blankenhorn, David. *Fatherless America: Confronting Our Most Urgent Social Problem.* New York: Basic, 1995.

Brotherson, Sean E., and Joseph M. White. *Why Fathers Count: The Importance of Fathers and Their Involvement with Children.* Harriman, TN: Men's Studies, 2007.

Calhoun, Adele Ahlberg. *Spiritual Disciplines Handbook: Practices That Transform Us.* Downers Grove: InterVarsity, 2005.

Canfield, Ken. *The Heart of a Father: How Dads Can Shape the Destiny of America.* Chicago: Northfield, 1996.

Carnes, Phillip Gene. "Like Sheep without a Shepherd: The Shepherd Metaphor and Its Primacy for Biblical Leadership." MA thesis, Reformed Theological Seminary, June 2007. Available at http://www.phillipcarnes.com/publications.

Carr, Johnny. *Orphan Justice: How to Care for Orphans beyond Adopting.* With Laura Captari. Nashville: Broadman & Holman, 2013.

Challies, Tim. *The Discipline of Spiritual Discernment.* Wheaton: Crossway, 2007.

Corbett, Steve, and Brian Fikkert. *When Helping Hurts: How to Alleviate Poverty without Hurting the Poor and Yourself.* Chicago: Moody, 2009.

Cockrel, Lisa Ann. "Solo Son." *Today's Christian Woman* 28.5 (2006) 56–59.

Croy, David Wyatt. "Sermon Notes." Communion Service, June 4, 1989. From the personal library of Dwight David Croy.

Croy, Dwight David. "Chaplain's Corner: We Cannot Fix the Unfixable without a Higher Power." *Arctic Warrior*, May 8, 2014. http://www.jber.af.mil/news/story.asp?id=123410256.

Dever, Mark. *What Is a Healthy Church?* Wheaton: Crossway, 2007.

Eldredge, John. *Fathered by God: Learning What Your Dad Could Never Teach You.* Nashville: Nelson, 2009.

Erickson, Beth M. *Longing for Dad: Father Loss and Its Impact.* Dearfield Beach, FL: Health, 1998.

Erickson, Millard. *Introducing Christian Doctrine.* Grand Rapids: Baker Academic, 2013.

Gorsuch, Geoff. *Brothers! Calling Men into Vital Relationships.* Colorado Springs: NavPress, 1994.

Hearne, Philip, and Gary Blackmon. "Lonely Sunday." Song. Candor, NC: self-produced, 2004.

Hughes, R. Kent. *Disciplines of a Godly Man.* Wheaton: Crossway, 2001.

Krause, Neal, and R. David Hayward. "Assessing whether Practical Wisdom and Awe of God Are Associated with Life Satisfaction." *Psychology of Religion and Spirituality* 7.1 (2014) 1–9. http://dx.doi.org/10.1037/a0037694.

Lieberman, Alicia F., et al. *Losing a Parent to Death in the Early Years: Guidelines for the Treatment of Traumatic Bereavement in Infancy and Early Childhood.* Washington, DC: Zero to Three, 2003.

Lupton, Robert D. *Compassion, Justice and the Christian Life: Rethinking Ministry to the Poor.* Ventura, CA: Regal, 2007.

———. *Toxic Charity: How Churches and Charities Hurt Those They Help and How to Reverse It.* New York: HarperOne, 2011.

MacDonald, Gordon. *Building Below the Waterline: Shoring Up the Foundations of Leadership.* Peabody: Hendrickson, 2011.

Mackey, Bonnie, and Wade Mackey. "Father Presence and Educational Attainment: Dad as a Catalyst for High School Graduations." *Education* 133.1 (2012) 139–50.

Mackey, Wade, and Ronald Immerman. "Cultural Evolution and the Nuclear Family: Whither Cleavage of the Father?" *Journal of Social, Evolutionary, and Cultural Psychology* 3.2 (2009) 155–81. http://psycnet.apa.org/journals/ebs/3/2/155.pdf&productCode=pa.

Manning, Brennan. *Abba's Child: The Cry of the Heart for Intimate Belonging.* Colorado Springs: NavPress, 2002.

Marche, Stephen. "Why Fatherhood Matters: Because Society Crumbles Without Us." *Esquire*, June/July 2013, 1–4. http://oweb.b.ebscohost.com.catalog.georgefox.edu.

McGeady, Mary Rose. *Sometimes God Has a Kid's Face.* Washington, DC: Covenant House, 2010.

McNulty, Paul J. "Natural Born Killers." *Policy Review* 71 (1995) 84–87.

Meade, Christopher P. *Leadership Alive: Changing Leadership Practices in the Emerging Twenty First Century Culture.* Boise: LeadershipAlive.com, 2008.

Miller, Donald. *Father Fiction: Chapters for a Fatherless Generation.* New York: Howard, 2010.

Oduyoye, Mercy Amba. *The Stones Will Cry Out: The Charism of the Voiceless.* Collegeville: Liturgical, 1990.

Osbeck, Kenneth W. *Amazing Grace: 366 Inspiring Hymn Stories for Daily Devotions.* Grand Rapids: Kregel, 2002.

Oxford, Linda K. "What Healthy Churches Do to Protect Vulnerable Others and Prevent Clergy Sexual Misconduct." *Family and Community Ministries* 25 (2012) 81–107.

Paddison, Angus. "The Authority of Scripture and the Triune God." *International Journal of Systematic Theology* 13.4 (2011) 448–62.

Payne, Ruby K. *A Framework for Understanding Poverty.* Highlands, TX: Aha! Process, 1996.

Peterson, William, and Ardythe Petersen. *The Complete Book of Hymns: Inspiring Stories about 600 Hymns and Praise Songs.* Carol Stream, IL: Tyndale, 2006.

Penner, Peter F. "Discerning and Following God's Mission." *Journal of European Baptist Studies* 4.2 (2004) 34–39.

Petty, Krista. "Fathering the Fatherless." *Journal of Family and Community Ministries* (Baylor University School of Social Work) 22 (2008) 41–44. http://www.baylor.edu/content/services/document.php/145479.pdf. 2007.

Rah, Soong-Chan. *Many Colors: Cultural Intelligence for a Changing Church.* Chicago: Moody, 2011.

Robinson, Monique. *Longing for Daddy: Healing from the Pain of an Absent or Emotionally Distant Father.* Colorado Springs: WaterBrook, 2004.

Sax, Leonard. *Boys Adrift: The Five Factors Driving the Growing Epidemic of Unmotivated Boys and Underachieving Young Men.* New York: Basic, 2007.

————. *Why Gender Matters: What Parents and Teachers Need to Know about the Emerging Science of Sex Differences.* New York: Three Rivers, 2005.

Sears, Alan, and Craig Osten. *The Homosexual Agenda: Exposing the Principal Threat to Religious Freedom Today.* Nashville: Broadman & Holman, 2003.

Shaw, Nathan. *Unto the Least of These: Expressing God's Love to Widows and the Fatherless.* Grand Rapids: Chosen, 2004.

Sowers, John. *Fatherless Generation: Redeeming the Story.* Grand Rapids: Zondervan, 2010.

Stafford, Wess. *Too Small to Ignore: Why the Least of These Matters Most.* Colorado Springs: WaterBrook, 2007.

Strong, James. *The New Exhaustive Concordance of the Bible.* Nashville: Nelson, 1996.

Strong, Mark E. *Church for the Fatherless: A Ministry Model for Society's Most Pressing Problem.* Downers Grove: InterVarsity, 2012.

Sweet, Leonard. *Nudge: Awakening Each Other to the God Who's Already There.* Colorado Springs: Cook, 2010.

Thomas, Pamela. *Fatherless Daughters: Turning the Pain of Loss into the Power of Forgiveness.* New York: Simon & Schuster, 2009.

Tolbert, La Verne. "The Relationship between Fatherless Children and Their Concept of the Fatherhood of God." *Lutheran Education* 139.3 (2010) 190–212.

US Census Bureau. "Living Arrangements of Children under 18 Years Old: 1960 to Present." July 1, 2012. https://www.census.gov/hhes/families/data/children.html.

Vitz, Paul C. *Faith of the Fatherless: The Psychology of Atheism.* San Francisco: Ignatius, 2013.

Woodley, Randy S. *Shalom and the Community of Creation: An Indigenous Vision.* Grand Rapids: Eerdmans, 2012.

Wytsma, Ken. *Pursuing Justice: The Call to Live and Die for Bigger Things.* Nashville: Nelson, 2013.

Yun, Brother. *The Heavenly Man: The Remarkable True Story of Chinese Christian Brother Yun.* Grand Rapids: Monarch, 2002.

Scripture Index

Old Testament

New Testament